SCATTERED THOUGHTS

DR. KRISHNA SAKSENA

PRABHAT
PAPERBACKS

Published by
PRABHAT PAPERBACKS
An imprint of Prabhat Prakashan Pvt. Ltd.
4/19 Asaf Ali Road,
New Delhi-110002 (INDIA)
e-mail: prabhatbooks@gmail.com

ISBN 978-93-5521-376-1
SCATTERED THOUGHTS
by Dr. Krishna saksena

Edition
First, 2023

Price
₹ 250 (Rupees Two Hundred Fifty Only)

Printed at
Impressions Printers, Sahibabad

Author's Note

This is a collection of essays by my close friend and colleague, Dr. Krishna Saksena. She is a distinguished teacher and scholar, has traveled widely and written several books including two novels, TAKE A U TURN and THE PRICE OF INNOCENCE and the autobiography, YOU ME AND THE DIVINE which were greatly appreciated by her readers. The essays in this volume are on a wide variety of topics ranging from love and family relationships to surgery and the present state of the country. Her style of presentation is unique: clear, straightforward, lively and forceful. She does well to illustrate her arguments with numerous examples, taken directly from her observation of people and situations she gained over many years. The reader will certainly find these essays instructive, thought-provoking and inspiring.

Introduction

This book is a presentation of myself as it shows my views and my inner self. I am deeply touched by the happenings around me. Present comes out of the past and gives a new direction to the future. I see traditions crumbling, values changing and new methods being adopted in society. I am elated to see the fast forward movement in technology and science but I am depressed at the faltering ways of living found in the new system of the society of today.

You can read the articles at random as they bear no connection to each other. The only remote connection can be that they are all the inner thoughts of one individual who has observed and reflected. My life has been one of turbulence, doubts and disappointments. I lost my husband when I needed him the most. I have been looking after a mentally challenged son for the last forty-five years of my life. A gloom surrounds me as I live alone with him now. The other children being happily married left to live at their different destinations. I had often cried within myself as I found life tiresome and defeating. I would have fallen down and finished myself in despair. But a strong hand lifted me up, the hand of the Divine, my Mother Divine. She gave me the strength to smile, to think positive and to live with hope, essentials to survive in this world.

I see around and observe that the world has drastically changed in the eighty-two years of my life that I have traveled so far. I feel highly disturbed and at times disgusted at events and men as I watch them helplessly. I become restless and often confused. Yet frustration and anger have never reached me to a point of desperation. I have seen in my life that hope had struggled out of discouragement and defeat. So also, I believe that a bright morning awaits us and not long a new horizon will greet us.

I thank all those who have helped me to bring out this small book. I am obliged to my colleagues, Prof. Dr. Sogani and Prof. Mrs. Leena Roy for giving their valuable comments. I am highly grateful to my younger son Bali Adawal, for giving his views on varied topics. I am indebted to my daughter Mangla for encouragement that she provides. But above all my special thanks go to my eldest son, Shankar Adawal who is the inspiration behind this book.

Krishna Saksena

Contents

Corruption

"Life is neither good nor an evil; it is simply the place where both exist." When evil overpowers good, then corruption sets in. In the olden days it is not that men with evil designs did not exist. They did, but the good and the honest far outnumbered them and so the society was not in danger. India has the privilege of having a rich spiritual background and a high sense of morality. It boasts of kings like Ram, Harish Chandra and Ashok. No one locked the house as he went out of the house. Honesty prevailed. There was almost no deceit and no wickedness. People lived an easy relaxed life.

Such things did not go on for long. Passing of time saw an utter neglect of the moral values that were once held high by the people. No more, any longer, men stuck to the norms taught by the sages of the old.

A man asked the sage,

"Should I give up everything like you if I have to live a life of honesty and truthfulness"?

The sage replied,

"Not at all. What you need to understand is that you can find peace and happiness only if you follow the path of unselfishness. If you are going to cling to your wealth, it is better you throw it away, than let it poison your heart. But if you do not cling to it and use it wisely, then you will be a blessing to the people."

"It is not wealth and power that make people corrupt but clinging to it."

There is a world of truth in what the sage said. What is important is to lead an ethical life of non-attachment. In no way it means that we give up all we have. Living in this world we need to live well, but our attachment should be with God. We can live in this world in the best possible way, but what is essential is that our focus should be on the Divine. Only then hearts can develop purity and an attitude of selfless service and a spirit of sharing with others. And this in fact was our dharma in the days of the past.

But now we have completely changed our direction from what we were once upon a time. Process, no doubt, has been gradual but corruption has gone deep within us and has taken the form of a disease that has spread all around in our Indian society. Now we are standing amongst the first few most CORRUPT countries of the world. What went wrong with us? Spiritually upright once, was it that we got mad after money and after power and lost all our moral sense?

In the last two decades of independence, India has seen a steep rise in the graph of the existing corruption. This issue has been highlighted by the public, the media and variety of forms of discussion and debates. All from the top to the bottom are neck deep buried in corruption. We stand and watch with disgust and anger. Why has this monster of corruption taken such a strong hold on us? The corrupt practices are now a part of our life style and we do not see anything wrong in it. A thought process has set in our minds that corruption has to be. It has become an essential part of our society. It is disgusting and disturbing as we begin to justify our corrupt ways. When we begin to think that there is nothing wrong in corrupt ways, I am sure, we have reached to a point of desperation which is the beginning of a disastrous end. There is no scope for correction if we understand that there is nothing wrong in being corrupt. In case we are honest, it is argued, we will be left far behind those whose success story has been due to their corrupt ways. Corruption has entered our minds and thoughts leading to corrupt the very spirit of the individual. Thus corrupt environment leads to corruption in society. Just madly running after power and money, which are our sole concern, we have all our ethical values. If you happen to have money and power, you are at the top, envied as considered the happiest. A young man when asked what he dreams to be, his quick retort was that he wished to become an Ambani.

If we look back, we find that there has been a continuous process of degeneration, ever since we started over looking our honest spiritual ways. Gautam Budha rightly said, "If you are going to cling to wealth and power, you are doomed. It is better to throw it away rather than poison your mind and heart." Since the time we neglected our honest spiritual ways, life has taken a turn. We prefer selfishness to selflessness, to service we prefer to boost our ego. Degeneration has set in and corruption is at the root of this magnum tree.

Some of the causes that have allowed corruption to grow so wild may be studied here:

Poverty

Poverty is one major cause of corruption in India. We have been independent for a long time. But no progress has been made in the direction of alleviating the poor of their poverty. India remains a country of the poor. All in the low ranks find it difficult to meet their both ends meet by the low scales of the payments that they receive. Left with no option, even the most honest succumb to corruption and take bribe wherever they can conveniently. I had an acquaintance, who would often give me lectures on honesty. I was amazed when I happened to visit her in her office and saw her taking bribes from all those who wanted their bills to be cleared fast. I looked at her with surprise, which she answered promptly, only avoiding to look into my eyes. "When I see my child dying because I cannot purchase costly essential medicines for her prescribed by the doctor, I falter and my sense of honesty gives way and my only concern remains how to make up the deficit and bring relief to my child. I am forced to adopt means which I would have otherwise resented." I heard her in silence and felt that to a great extend poverty does lead one to adopt corrupt ways. See the head clerk who would keep on avoiding your file to move on to the other table, till in desperation you give him his share. Think of the police who stops you as you rush on, crossing despite red light, but soon allows you to move on with a smile if you quietly pass on some cash. They all argue, being ill paid they had to adopt means to recover and somehow maintain their families. Even an attendant sitting at the door of an officer will refuse you entry unless few notes are passed on to him. When you give him his share, you are ushered in with a bow and a smile. Immediate need of money is definitely more important and pressing than ethical and moral values.

Lack of Accountability

There is a need for an efficient system of accountability. A strong machinery to keep an eye on those who indulge in corrupt practices would have helped to control corrupt ways adopted by the individuals and groups. The absence of a strong system, to keep an eye on the crime, has given rise and an encouragement to corrupt practices. Corrupt practices continue to grow unabated. Matters have gone so bad that one shudders to think of it.

A group of policemen were sitting and chatting:

"This system of accountability is so efficient in England that they can find out the culprit within a few days."

"How long?" asked the other.

"Oh within a week", he replied.

"In America the system is still better", said the third.

"How?" one in the group enquired.

"They find out the culprit within two days", answered his friend. One who was quietly listening to this discussion remarked:

"You are fools. We, in India are far more advanced."

"How?" All looked at him with surprise as they all wanted the answer.

"Because we know well about the crime a few hours even before it is committed." He answered staring at them and looking serious.

You need not laugh, for it is no joke. Here are those who are held to account for a crime join hands with those who commit the crime. We need to hang our heads in shame to see this state of corruption that exists here. Corruption, the great giant, has gripped us so strongly that it is rampant everywhere, to the entire length and breadth of our social fabric and has gone deep down to the deepest of levels.

Economic Disparity

In India, there are two distinct classes. On the one hand are those who have immense wealth, while on other side are those that do not have even enough money to afford a proper living. With the passage of time the rich are growing richer every day while the poor are being pushed down each moment. The rich can offer bribes and get their work, legal or illegal, done with great ease and surety. They can mint money because corruption easily allows them to do so. The poor stands aghast as he watches the situation with despair. Disgusted with corrupt ways from top to the bottom his only consolation is to blame his destiny. Without the backing of money all his sincere and hard work yields no results. He is short of money and cannot offer bribes, without which he languishes in poverty. Money is God !

Poor Legal System

Our legal system is such that it takes a long, a very long time for one to get justice. It is rightly said that justice delayed is justice denied. The long interval helps the one with money to bribe the judge, to make the witness change his version and to bring up new evidences. Money power can achieve the impossible. Poor can be punished for no crime of his while the rich walks out with all charges falsified. With pride he moves in society as a respectable man even after committing the most heinous crime. Court dates come after very long intervals, public memory is very short, the lengthy duration takes away the sharpness of the crime. Many cases of those who can afford to fill the pockets are declared "closed" because of the want of evidence. But a poor robber whose crime was that he had stolen only rupees 200 to save his child from dying languishes in jail for 3 years. He was given 2 years imprisonment for the crime committed, but the judgment came so late that he had already served in jail for 3 years. How just is our legal system!

Wrong Evaluation

Money power is to be noticed everywhere. The tragedy of the situation is that it is being utilized for personal benefits at wrong places. The influence can be seen even where merit has to be chosen. A poor boy, intelligent, hardworking and with a meritorious record has no chance to be chosen for a post where in the interview he stands with a son of a rich man though he has no merit. This brings about lot of discontent. But this is the part of life and one must learn to bear it.

Morally and ethically weak

Once, we Indians, were proud of our character. Money was utilized for the good of all. People had learnt to suffer if that would give happiness to others. Service, not selfishness was the motto. It is no longer so. Now the rule is "Me and Mine". All else needs to be forgotten. Our ethics, our self-respect, our love for human values and our love for our men and motherland have all been thrown to the winds.

Corruption is to be seen from the highest level to the lowest level. If those standing at the top had shown some honesty, there was some hope. But unfortunately it is those at the top, the privileged, the wealthy and the influential that are the ones that hardly allow any space for honesty to persist in any other layer of society. Corruption in fact animates from them. Corruption goes to all levels and in all spheres of activities. The politicians, our so called leaders and well-wishers are corrupt and encourage the bureaucrat to be corrupt. From the senior bureaucrats, slowly and steadily corruption has come down to the lowest levels of functionaries.

Today we are standing at the threshold of a new millennium with Indian National Congress and many other parties without a single leader of the stature of Gandhi, Sardar Patel or Subhash Chandra Bose. Today the sets of politicians of all political parties are just money making parties.

The vision of a great India is lost somewhere. If Mahatma Gandhi would come alive and see this India, corrupt from top to bottom bringing the country down to a dismal state, he would collapse with pain and remorse. Did he ever even in his dream envisaged this India? He said that the heart of India is in the villages and in an independent India he would like each and every villager to be happy. He should be with his smiling family and proud of his blooming farms. Children growing up with free and good medical facilities and equally efficient education provided to them by the government. Tears come even in our eyes as we see farmers committing suicide one after the other. Under corrupt governments farmers are seen reeling under heavy loads of debts, their children doomed, running to cities to find some employment to give relief to their parents and families and their lands grabbed under some flimsy pretext. What a tragedy!!

The ugliest face of corruption here in India is that our Congress party which worked to oust the foreigners has installed a foreigner to rule. We have lost all our sense of self-respect. This party is now presenting a dismal picture. Today the politicians are no longer dedicated souls, they are merely selfish money making characters. There is no leader of the stature of Lal Bahadur Shastri. Corruption is now like a drug without which the addicts find it difficult to survive. It has become a way of life and to uproot it appears to be a herculean task. It requires an iron hand to deal with this problem.

The cleansing must start from the top echelons of society. As soon as we see a big name involved in a case of corruption, there is lot of noise made for some time, but with the passage of time it dies out and corruption goes unabated. All those at the clearing end are bought by the power of money. Even the investigating agencies supposed to be independent are working at the orders of the ruling parties. Surely no damage can be done to the so called high ups. No breakthrough can be achieved in any scam. The high ups cannot be touched and the lower ones are sheltered by them. So things remain and corruption stands supreme. I happen to speak to a district supply officer who was suspended twice for taking bribes but reinstated with promotion every time. He happened to be a close acquaintance of mine, so he talked freely.

"How do you manage to take bribes yet left with honour?" I asked. "Ah, I do not have to ask for it, so how can I be held guilty", he replied with confidence. "You get without asking?" I asked much to my surprise.

"Our shares are fixed right from the minister to the dealing clerk. I get my due". He spoke calmly.

"But how is it that you are the one who is always caught and then left?" I asked.

“Because I am the one who is directly dealing with the public and so they go and report against me. For the show of justice I am suspended”, he replied.

“And then?” I asked .“What then?” I am left on the plea that “no evidence was found against me”. “What about your promotion?” I asked.

“That is the prize for keeping my mouth shut and not talking about others involved”, he answered with a naughty smile.

I am quite surprised to see how the things are moving up in our land. Our love and dedication for our mother land is lost somewhere in the last sixty years of independence. Today we are standing bereft of a single leader dedicated to the nation and its people. Integrity and honesty are nowhere to be seen. All politicians of various parties are just working to establish estates for themselves and for their seven generations to come. Political parties, following the congress, have no goals, no ethics, and no ideologies. Multi scams are coming out one after the other. Crores and crores of money is wasted in constructing bridges and buildings, in organizing gaines and in starting the telecom sector. Dishonesty prevails at all levels. The politicians encourage the bureaucrats to be corrupt and in return the bureaucrats have enjoyed the protection of the politician, in all their nefarious activities. All are incorrigible and all that we can do is to watch all this with disgust and anger. No breakthrough can be done because it is the high ups who are responsible and involved and they cannot be touched. Multi crores of the nation, which belongs to the poor of the country is siphoned off outside the country. What can be done when protectors themselves become criminals? When those at the top cannot be brought to books, how can there be any cleansing at the bottom?

It would be doing great injustice if those at the lower rungs of the ladder are punished and those sitting at the top are allowed to bask in the sunshine of their riches and power. We well know who all are corrupt but the irony of the system is that they cannot be touched. How are the things to go on like this? Is there no way out of this tragic situation that we are in?

Corruption that emanates from the top and permeates to the lowest levels goes on unchecked and is sucking the very blood of the nation. Each individual realizes that he is in the grip of corruption somehow or the other.

Does Anna Hazare, who symbolizes anti-corruption mood of the people and his woes, raise some hope for the future? For a better INDIA? Let us wait and watch.

❑

A Wake-up Call for the Nation

My father was a great educationist. He would often tell me that in anything that we do, there ought to be a purpose. Education which builds up a child and gives him a direction ought to be taken very seriously. It has to be considered as very important and needs to have a right approach. A nation's welfare depends upon it. It is here that character is formed. Education is a very vital problem, of which we have to take up the responsibility. If we are going down today, it can be traced to the wrong approach that is being made to education.

Let us first understand the purpose of education. Apart from teaching specific skills which, no doubt, is important, it builds up the character and imparts knowledge and wisdom. It develops in an individual the quality to make right judgments. When knowledge or wisdom is absent, facts can be misused. If there is a balance such a situation does not arise. A balanced view can take so many aspects into account. This can only be provided by the right type of education. And it need not be emphasized that on education rests our culture, our entire make up by which a nation is known.

So education should have a top priority. It ought to be considered as something sacred. A uniformed, innocent child is given to be molded. From three years when a child joins a school, to eighteen years when he leaves, he is passing through a very critical period, a most impressionable period of his life.

Impressions formed during this period last long and make the man. To make one as a useful member of a society, it all depends on how education is imparted.

Education needs to build up a close relationship between the teacher and the taught. The process of building up closeness between the students and the teacher goes much beyond the boundaries of the classroom or learning period. It is a process of developing a relationship of trust, faith, respect and honour. Rightly cultivated here, it blossoms in all directions and varied facets of life.

Education ought not to be taken as a 'system' but must be treated as a process as real as living as growing up. A child is being educated right from the time of his birth and it continues to the time of his death. The formal education is but a phase in this spectrum of ongoing education and ought to be developed in a way to bring about an integration of the entire process. It needs to give a strong support to the whole process. A child may have many teachers, like parents, family elders around, friends and enemies But the one that makes major impact and makes him the man that he has to be is the education at school. Once because of high fever my own 5 year child, going into semi-consciousness, did not ask for me but kept on shouting for his class teacher.

Before it gets too late, the current education needs to be corrected. An unbalanced focus is laid on skills, at the neglect of the other very important issues. The relationship between the teacher and the taught shares no closeness of understanding and love. A teacher is considered as one who is just doing a job for the money it brings. Beyond that there is nothing for him. The students look down upon the teacher as paid employee, as one who has failed to make up for higher and better jobs. The teacher is nothing beyond this.

A complete breakdown in values has overtaken the sacred link that once bound the teacher and the taught. When there is no closeness of understanding, no faith and respect for the teacher, the student gets just the cold facts without any feeling of realization. On the part of the teachers, they have absolutely lost the interest in the development and welfare of the students. It is no longer for them a mission, a calling that would influence the future generations. Thus the sacred bond that existed between them is broken and the sufferer is the nation at large.

Where then have we gone wrong? Current education has absolutely missed its goal primarily for the reason that our focus has gone towards a wrong direction. What we are giving importance to have brought ourselves down in our own estimation and we are fast moving towards the brink of disaster. We might have risen outwardly in the eyes of the other nations, but we have lost our very spirit. We are like unbalanced individuals, who are being controlled by friends fashion, public opinion, popular individuals or ideas, carnal lusts of the flesh, or by other externals such as money and things.

Our present education is too much focused on skills, very little on anything else. There is no relationship built between the teacher and the student. Teachings can only flow over the conduit of respect and faith. Otherwise all that comes is merely cold facts with no realization. Teaching should be made a calling, a mission to influence the generation that has still to come. Too much of competition saps away the pleasure of learning and discovering new things. Students study simply from one exam to another. Focus is on getting marks, everything else is subordinate. A successful student to the means one who is getting degrees that would land him into high posts that would give him money. It is good to make money and all that money can buy, but they fail to check up what they have lost, which no amount of money can buy. Money may be the husk of many things, but not the kernel." We are told that "if money is lost nothing is lost, but if the character is lost everything is lost." Yet money stands supreme and we aim to get the maximum. Education is no longer a stepping stone towards bringing out strong characters. Thus the saying is just a thing to repeat.

Too much of competitiveness saps away the pleasure of learning and discovering new things. Students only bother to get out of one exam to another. Concentration is only on getting more and more marks, which become the be-end of their educational career, everything else is incidental. The impact of all this on our educational system is to bring forth people who are trained to think within narrow confines. They never develop a real taste of what they have studied. In real life, such people just become followers and can never become thinkers and leaders and philosophers.

The young age is that of carefree enjoyment, whether it is in studies or it is in plays. But now the burden of books and the load of parrot-like memorizing take away from them all the joy with which they can learn and grow. Too much focus on results makes them unaware of the pleasures of studying. They are no longer thinkers. But a vibrant society needs to think out of the box, who have the confidence to challenge the system and improve upon it. All that we are producing are followers who are simply striving to make more and more money as the ultimate goal of life. A student no longer thinks or acts according to divinely inspired ideals.

What then is the solution? How about bringing a change in the process?

We must understand the real purpose of education and then strive to achieve it. Education ought to be made less competitive and more of fun. Through playfulness and ease we can make the students grasp things that we may never dream of. Too many subjects, with little knowledge about each absolutely confuse them and make them feel that their task is too burdensome.

Examinations ought not to be the only criteria of passing judgment on a student. A day to day assessment ought to be made for the final analysis of a child. To give inspiration, creativity ought to be awarded. Ingenuity must be given a boost by recognition. A new spirit ought to be instilled that would make them to think individually and out of the strict confines.

Basic primary education ought to be made free and compulsory for all. That was Gandhiji's dream for an independent India and it is a shame that after so many years of independence it still remains a dream. It is high time that we should wake up to understand the importance of education for one and all.

It should be very clear that higher education is not meant for all. There are those who are fit for technical education. Yet there are others who are suited for non-technical branches. Accordingly looking into their aptitude and fitness, while making assessment, the students must be allowed only to join those various branches of education, for which they have aptitude and skill. Let us not allow to fit square pegs in round holes. All this is only possible if a close watch is kept on the development of a child and it is taken care to make him grow in a branch that would suit his taste, his temperament, his aptitude and his skill for his full growth.

The present education which is highly objective seems to be turning out those who know how to tick on 'yes' or 'no'. Thus passing out of school, they do not know how to write an application correctly and give out their thoughts lucidly on any subject whatsoever. They might have gained information, but at the cost of knowledge. Educationists are happy that they have expanded their circle of information tremendously, but they are unaware of great loss. They are turning out students who have no confidence in their own selves on the knowledge gained. The loss is tremendous and needs to be attended to immediately.

To meet all this, education ought to be treated as a challenge before it gets too late, Teachers ought to be trained. They ought to be made to feel that their mission is sacred and on which lies the hopes of a nation. They should stop feeling that they are there to instruct but must understand that they are there to teach, to mould, to make them grow by their words and by their examples. Love has power, the power to create. It is this power that they must possess. If our expectations emerge from love, we become masters of our expectations. In this world of cut-throat competition, it is to the teacher that we look for a change. Their noble profession needs to be treated with respect. They ought to be well paid so that they can succeed in doing their work with honesty. Their welfare and needs ought to be taken in account so that they are in a position to give out their best.

No education can be complete if it fails in its primary job of character building. The school curriculum must include a period where the students are taught the traditions of a country to which they belong. India has the tradition that is rich, respect for the elders, a spirit to share, a feeling of co-operation, oneness with all rich and poor, and a sense of honesty. These must be emphasized and brought about in a student before he leaves the school. The feeling that money is God needs to be replaced by values that go to enrich a character. All students are alike, rich or poor, and if there is any difference it is in their intelligence, diligence and in their free thinking.

All education must make them understand the divinity that is within them. They must rise up to realize this. All education should clearly state in non-sectarian way the importance of morality and religion. These are the most important aspects of life and should be carefully cultivated in all students.

A school would then turn out those, though skilled will be rich in honesty and dedication. A spirit needs to be developed in a child when he understands that there are those around him from whom he can draw lessons. His first teachers are his family members and his parents, then those who guide him in school, also there are elders around him, and then his peers and his friends and his enemies. He must welcome lessons from any direction. A spirit of humility should overtake him and not of pride that would tell him that what he knows and what he is, he is great. Knowledge ought to be welcomed from any direction, for it is gold.

A grave responsibility rests on the shoulders of our educationists. With a correct and a systematic approach, we shall be turning out those who are skilled but are rich in dedication and honesty. No longer then would be corrupt politicians who come with promises only to fill their own pockets. There would be no more officers working on bribes. Instead there would be individuals who can think broadly, who have the spirit to share and help those in need. Generally there would be an adherence to the ideals of our nation. We shall then have no longer newspapers filled with incidences that give us shocks after shocks. No longer there would be those who have forgotten their own culture and are imitating the westerners in dress, looks and lust. We consider Tsunami a great tragedy. But we are not ashamed of a greater tragedy of illiteracy. We are adhering to the wrong principles of education that is taking the nation astray.

❑

Hullo Mom

Shashi was proud of her three sons, Ram, Shyam and Gautam as she saw them growing up, tall, handsome and strong. They were intelligent, hardworking and good in academics. Often she would laugh heartily as she would tell them, "You are fortunate that you have this 'mean' mother". Her strict principles and harsh simple ways of living would often annoy the sons. But then they had to listen and follow her ways. She had no bank balance to help her sons. But she gave them what she got from her father, discipline, selflessness and honesty.

They grew up, getting distinction in their fields of study, and finally getting into good jobs. Shashi lost her husband, which was a great blow to her, but never for a moment, she had a feeling of insecurity for she had the strength and support of her three sons behind her. The sons got married and were on in their search for better jobs and better lives. Often the wives would get annoyed at their ways of thinking and style of living. But for the sons it was hardly a matter of concern.

They did well in their jobs and soon they were offered good positions outside the country. The three thought and thought over it and wondered if they could leave the old and helpless mother. They were her strength. A battle was on in each one of them, a battle between two opposite forces; one of faith, peace, humility and joy that comes out of serving selflessly and the other that afforded them money, position, greed and ego. The battle between the two opposite forces rattled within them and they were restless.

They came to take the mother's view. She told them, "In the long run it is you who will shape your lives. My work is over. I have given you a shape that I liked. But now that you have grown up, it is your responsibility, of what you make out from what you have learnt from me. This process has to go on till the time of your death. Remember the choice that you will make will decide your happiness. You need not grumble. If the decision you take is wrong, there is something left definitely wrong in you."

Finally while Ram, the eldest decided to stay back, as his mother's teaching had gone down deep within him, the younger two Shyam and Gautam decided to run after more money, more power, and more comforts. Both departed with their families. They came to say good-bye to their mother and take her blessings. As the mother put her trembling hand on their heads, she looked lost and disappointed yet she managed to forge a smile on her face. She saw her own words thrown to the dust, as she had often told her sons, "Be eager to serve, to come to the rescue of others." They had forgotten the principle of right living. They were the strength of their weak mother, but they withdrew for their own selfish interests. The mother had learnt well by this time that she had not to demand but accept what comes on her way. This change of attitude had made her life easy and satisfied. If her dreams were shattered she knew, that there was something wrong in her upbringing. Leaving all else, money, money, money that was what that made their world go. Quietly she sighed.

The eldest son, Ram. took charge of his mother, not at all with a feeling of grudge but with a feeling of elation. He took his mother's hand and said, "Cheer up, Mom, you will always find Ram by your side." The bright foreign offers had little meaning for him, for he could get good position anywhere but he very much preferred the happiness of his mother. He had a small decent house comprising of four rooms out of which a small room was made ready for the mom.

His mother was his greatest concern and small jobs that he could do for her gave him immense joy. In the morning, he would come and greet her with the words of “Jai Mata”. He would then lift her up, giving her the support of his strong hands. He would then take her to the toilet and bring her back to her bed. She would then comfortably sit on her bed and get ready for her meditation and jap. After two hours Ram would enter the room carrying two cups of tea to sit by her side and enjoy her company. So the day would start with a pleasant note.

Before leaving for the office, Ram would usually peep into the mother’s room and finding her looking at him, he would stop and ask her if she needed anything from the market. On her shaking her head with a smile, he would give back a smile and move off. The daughter-in law would then take charge and in time gave her breakfast and lunch.

On his return from his office, he would often find her stitching and humming a tune. Ram would tease her, on which she would reply proudly, “Once I sang in concerts and on stage. but now my voice quivers and I sing only one song”. “Which song, Mom”. “O, it was your dad’s favourite”. “Now sing that song for me,” Ram would insist and then she would sing with mouth smiling but eyes moistened with tears,

Nobody knows the trouble I see,

Nobody knows my sorrow.

Sometimes I am up, sometimes I am down,

Sometimes I am almost to the ground.

Oh! Yes my Lord.

“It is a lovely song. Continue with it.” Ram would insist on Mom, and plead “Let me be a part of it.” Mom would then take Ram’s hand and look at him with deep sympathy.

Whenever Ram would see his mom massaging her legs, he would immediately come forward, made her to lie down and start giving the massage to her. She gave the return by her sweet smile. While doing massage Ram would remind his mom, "You remember, mom, we three had our turns for massaging your legs when we were young and whenever it was my turn I would run off and hide in myself. You were then very angry with me. Now, mom, you see I am making up for all those turns." He would laugh mischievously and make the mother also laugh.

Such were the days they passed together. If the mother would look sick, he was depressed and took her to the doctor immediately. He was always asking, "Did you sleep well? Did you take the food properly?" Every night he would make it a point to come to his mother's room, see if she had gone off to sleep, and cover her lovingly with a sheet. While doing so, he would glance at her face and every wrinkle there would bring forth a thousand memories in his mind.

Time kept on running fast. Her two other sons rang her up now and then to enquire about her welfare. While ending their calls, they were sure to say, "take care". Meaningless words, that sounded so jarring to the mother. Gradually both made lot of money, though it still remained insufficient for them to meet their ever increasing demands. One fine day Shyam called up his mother and said, "Mom, I love you and I want you to shift to a spacious kothi consisting of ten rooms which I am arranging for all of you." The mother smiled and told him, "I shall let you know about it tomorrow." When Ram came to sit by her side, she told him what Shyam had said. Ram replied, "Mom, have you forgotten what you told about yourself? You were brought up with so many brothers and sisters only in two rooms and that was responsible for sowing within you all a spirit of understanding, love and co-operation, which brought you all so close to each other, a feeling that exists even today. So many rooms will only isolate us all. Then there will be the problem of maintenance and cleanliness." Next day the mother told Shyam, "Thank you, beta, that you thought of me and my comforts. That is like a great son.

But today I do not need more than one small room for myself. So many rooms will only puzzle me. I have now no strength to move about freely. I am always looking for someone to help me."

After few days Gautam came on a visit to see his mother. He was puzzled by the pollution in the air. He talked about the corruption that is with the Indians. Indiscipline and dishonesty disgusted him. He, now could not breathe in such an atmosphere. "All is very true", replied his mom "but what have you done? Only to leave your mother and your motherland and get settled in a foreign country to enjoy that which never belonged to you and then to denounce what is your very own." Gautam was silent and felt a little ashamed of himself.

He went back to U.S. and after few months he gave a call to his mom, "Ma, I am arranging a car of the latest model so that you can comfortably move about here and there." This time Shashi did not ask for the time to think about but replied instantly, "Thank you Beta, for thinking of me so kindly. I am happy that sometimes you remember me. But my sonny, one who had spent all her life traveling in crowded buses, at times hanging on the door needs no such luxury. Now I do not go out much as I have grown so old and so feeble. I prefer to stay at home to do puja, read books and enjoy the company of my dear Ram and my grandchildren."

Time passed on happily with Ram by her side. They would share numerous memories both sweet and sour. Ram would often notice the tears that numbed her eyes. Ram, in India, not only earned money but acquired a good position in society. He would often discuss with his mom about people and take clue from her vast experience. She would give her advice, "Beta the power is not in money but in making the lives of the people around a little better." He always respected her wishes and was ready to give a helping hand to others. He gave and forgot, without ever expecting any returns. He did good deeds that benefited the people. He saved some from humiliation, some from depression and was always willing to hear the woes of others. A great soul, who believed always what his mother told him, "Joy comes back doubly if you give joy to others." He could make his mother smile and that was what brightened his life.

A small child never cares about his dress or his possessions. For him, his greatest gift is his mother. A smile from her, cheers him up and he forgets all his worries. He willingly takes her hand that is extended to support him. Her lap is the child's heaven. When one day the mother gets old and feeble, all that she needs is a kind loving support from his child and nothing else. A word of sympathy, an assuring smile, a strong hand brought forward to hold her and a little concern that must come out of his love and considerations. Are the children willing to give a bit of what she has given in abundance? Think and reflect and give the answer to yourself.

The mother finally came to the day when she had to take leave from all. As she lay in her bed surrounded by her relations, sons and friends one could see her eyes searching for someone so special to her. And only when her son Ram came forward and put his hands round her neck and lifted her up slightly, her eyes all of a sudden brightened with a new wonderful gleam that was never seen before. She was speechless but her smiling eyes said to her son in a clear loud tone, "Beta, I never said thank you to you as I said to my other two sons. But believe me, Ram, every breath of mine has blessed you. Rest assured that my spirit will ever continue to bless you." As Ram kissed the mother, she quietly closed her eyes. Ram laid her down on the bed. He then sat down beside her and with folded hands he prayed to her:

Colour me now,
Before you leave me,
Colour me with
Your song
Colour me in
Your secret melody

Colour me in
The light of your laughter
Colour me with
Kindness of your tears
May your colour
Colour my very soul ... (Tagore)

Tears rolled down the cheeks of her dear sonny, Ram as he put the mother on the ground. He then ran out fast to relieve himself from the pain of parting. The mother had nothing precious to leave, no bank balance, no property and no ornaments. But what was really precious to Ram were her favourite books and her writings. He took them all with reverence and placed them in a small almirah. On the top of it, he placed his mother's photograph and garlanded it. A small lamp, he placed before it, which with its brightness tore the darkness of the room. He then glanced at his mother and told her never to leave his side and always continue to guide him.

Shashi, at least, had one such son who well knew his responsibility. I wonder and pity the lot of those mothers who are devoid of any such support. They are left alone, at the mercy of others, or perhaps at the mercy of their rich sons who have gone and settled abroad and feel more than satisfied if they could provide the parents with kothi and cash. We often read in the newspapers how such parents are robbed and murdered. In a land whose culture has produced sons like Sravan Kumar whose services offered to the parents have become an example, we have now sons who in their selfishness, pride and greed forget their mothers and their happiness. A mother, stands as the highest symbol of selfless love and sacrifice. In the worst of circumstances she will never curse her child. How then are the sons reacting? Have they lost their souls? One who gave them life has no meaning for them. Think seriously before it gets too late. Mother will forgive you but God will never do so. The Indian sons are forgetting that the dignity of human race is founded on the very principle that "life is to give". What can then help us to turn the tide in another direction? Technical education, and brilliance in skill cannot achieve the desired goal. A turn to spiritualism is the need of the hour, wherein one learns to work for the welfare of others. If they have to escape from their "littleness" they must turn to hear the words of Zarathustra: "Seek your happiness in the happiness of all, and regard the sufferings of others as your own and hasten to assuage them."

❑

Lust and Love

"Impart sex education to teenagers, so that they do not indulge in pre-mature sex." This is the advice to the ministry of education and to the parents given only few days back by a session court judge, Justice Dharmesh Sharma, while he sentenced a 22year man for rigorous imprisonment and fine. It punished the accused for establishing a sexual relationship with a teen age girl, though they were friends. The whole problem is that sex has become a vital part of society. It is a part of enjoyment. It is as good as going out on a picnic, or shopping or sight-seeing.

Rupa at the tender age of 14 found no problem in kissing or necking her boyfriend. The mother did not like this and objected, the daughter coolly replies,

"What is wrong with you, Mom. There is no harm as we are friends."

"But there are other ways of expressing your friendship" the mother suggested.

"You seem to be living in the age of Sita and Ram. You are not running with times." Rupa gives a quick reply.

The poor mother is stunned and remains quiet and disturbed. The husband also tells her to move with times.

By the age of seventeen, the young are good enough for further body contacts. Ramesh brought his girlfriend home. The parents were happy to talk to her. Even they asked her to come over for lunch. But they were shocked, when she stayed back and both locked themselves in a room and spent an hour there together. When she came back to say good-bye they gave a sour look and did not speak to her. They were tight-lipped when the son came to sit with them. The parents thought that any adverse comment may put a dent on their own relationship.

For youngsters of the day, sex is not a problem for coming into relationship. They try sex to check out their physical compatibility before they would allow the relationship to go forward. So sex remains no longer a matter of heart but of head. Intelligence has to be used for coming together. The heart has no place.

"He seems to bore me with his lazy and clumsy physical approach. So I have decided to leave this fellow and move on to the next." This is what Tanya told her friend Anju.

"Oh, my Gaurav is so exciting in his advances that I love to be with him and move forward in our relationship." Sapna confided in her friend Anju.

The youngsters explore all devices in sex to be smart when in company. It is this compatibility that makes them to move forward. Sex is the touchstone for all relationships. This is true with an elderly lady as well with a girl of tender age.

To spice the love-life the young try all means to look attractive and sexy. They get saucy hot chocolate waxes. The dresses are kept short and the open legs are tidied up with cocoa waxes and scented oils. They take special care to brush their teeth before going out to make sure that they do not have bad breath. The dresses are designed in a manner to show the body. All methods are tried to look really sexy. On this road should the boys be left behind? The saloons are ready to do their best for them. All this to make them run after each other!!

An agency man who met me recently, told me that sex is the burning topic of the day. It has become not only important but an essential part of the people. So many queries on sex problems keep on coming from all quarters that they get tired of responding to them. Sex is no longer a topic to feel shy about, or to keep it in a closet. Elderly women continue to chat with young boys on the facebook to soon come together. Just imagine a young boy coming to a woman of the age of his mother! She is obliged by the young, who in return goes away with rich gifts.

From the tender to the old, all are crazy about sex. The culture of the day takes all steps forward to enhance it and make it more convenient by its new devices of condoms and special pills. The mother allows the daughter to go out with boys. She tries her best to give it a cover of decency by allowing her to go when there are other girls too going in the party. But she is well aware of what goes there.

A young man picks up his girlfriend from her office and takes her to a shopping spree and then brings her home where the wife is waiting for him since long. They take tea together and then the young man walks to the other room accompanied by his girlfriend, close the door from inside and have a good sexy session. All this under the very nose of his wife! In the meantime some acquaintance nocks at the door. She runs to tell him:

"He has still not returned from the office." Poor thing, all this to save his and her own honour!

When the friend goes away the wife says,

"My dear, I do not mind as long as you do all this outside the house. But it is too much to bear it at home."

The husband replied, "How sad! you do not allow me space in my very house. You get your share from me, so you need not stop me to have my full. If you do not like this, you may do whatever you like."

Thus sex has assumed a place of great importance for all, young, old, married or unmarried and for any and every age whatsoever. It is playing a pivotal role in the modern society.

A young girl goes through three to four such experiences before she settles down. She is careful enough not to mention the previous experiences to the next, but in case it is found out by her boyfriend and he questions:

"I heard you were going about with Arun for a long time?" tells Piyush.

"Oh! that boy was mad for me and was running after me, but I refused to give him any lift. His very presence annoyed me, as his body gave out a repelling smell."

So the matter was decided between the two. Sex, as time is moving on, no longer remains the domain of the elders and grown-ups. It is now a passion, a reality with the young.

At times the girl confides in her boyfriend

"I have been going about with Anant, but somehow I could not carry on for long." Says Priti to Akash.

And when somebody asked Akash "How is it you are going on with that bitch, when you well know about her." The reply comes, "I do not care for her past as long as she is loyal to me." They go on with each other with comfort on assurances.

So youngsters go about, girls and boys, and have great fun. Cafes, campuses, malls and cinema houses are full with their shouts and laughter. They are overjoyed and full of smiles, they move about hand in hand, without shyness, and with pride.

The one while being involved in high sexual activity, cries out, "I love you" and soon comes the response from the other, "I love you too." Is love to be equated to lust and passion? They will soon be sharing the bed again with someone else, uttering the same words again and again. Is love so cheap? Love is equated to God. But with the people today love is not a matter of heart. It is a matter of their intelligence. This sex game may appear very sweet for the time being as all sweet words are attached to it. But understanding what love is one has to go deep into the word and give it a serious thought.

Love is seen in Krishna's relationship with Radha. Here there is no sexual tinge. Only the souls mingle. Krishna exhorts us to engage with the world romantically, understanding well that romance is not just an amorous activity but sweet love. "This love is to be understood, to be expressed and experienced equally through the enjoyment of luxuriance of the world of blossoms and birds, the fertility and fecundity of the world around us, and above all our engagement with our fellow beings. And all this by indulging the world of our senses and affirming an emotional oneness of the world around us." (Osho)

Love and lust may be compared. Both are state of mind emotion. In love the focus is on the other. In lust the focus is on yourself and your pleasure. Lust is so self-centered that it even neglects the stipulation of decency, the norms of society and the regulations of scriptures. While love is about giving, lust is about taking. While love submits itself to all rules and regulations, lust rejects for its own hedonistic pleasure. Sex that is unregulated, whimsical, immoral and irreligious is the direct result of lust.

We have many living examples of what love really means. Heer-Ranjha, Lailla-Majnu, Saleem-Anarkali are few that needs mention here. Love never knows what it gains. It sacrifices even life at its alter. It rises much above sex. Sex may be the outcome of love but never the cause of it. This is our Indian culture. Culture, by the present young generation is treated as an ornament. It seems no longer to be an expression of a nation's character. We, Indians, believe in right living. Have we lost all our sense of responsibilities? In many ways even the West has envied our system. They have begun to feel that arranged marriages are better than theirs based on sexual appearances, when broken marriages is the common theme of their society.

We have been proud of our culture, but it seems we are ending up by imitating the West and their ways. For this we are getting proud of. There are some restless elements that cannot stand the shameless sex outbursts on friendship day and become violent. They are also not right in their actions of beating the girls. For such actions cannot change the society. Sex game may appear very sweet for the time being, but afterwards, I am sure, the mouth shall be filled with gravel. Separations, broken marriages are the result of sex games. It is the ego that is heightened and all other feelings forgotten. The modern youth is running after small transitory satisfaction. What a waste as the pleasure passes before the smile. Finally they discover that love under the umbrella of marriage is the most difficult way to purify the heart. Getting too attached to sex, they forget the ultimate results and suffer. It is like enjoying the outer husk of a cocoanut, the tasteless part of it, while overlooking its inner substance, which is the delicious core.

Relationships are meant to generate more love and not to intensify the ego in a person. The society is geared by technological advancement, taking all to new shores of amusement, entertainment, communication, the principle tenets of love and relationship are forgotten. The love we have in our youth is superficial compared to the love of an old man for his rugged, old wife, in whose wrinkles he remembers with love the time that he had spent with her. Faithfulness, love unto death, is their duty towards each other. How long and how far does the sex stand?

What to say of youngsters, the elders too stand in the same line of sex, passion and lust. Famous singer, Ali, says "I am not suited for one marriage" and he continues to say "I am a free spirit." He wonders "what happens when you meet a new situation, and are faced with temptation." The temptation comes in the form of passion and lust. The singer goes from one to the other and may even to the third as his father tells us. In order to hide his passion and give it a good name, he goes about marrying again and again and says "I love you all." Is this the definition of love? Marriages to cover your temptation, passion and lust can never be equated to love. Love requires dedication, sacrifice, and a curb to all temptations whatsoever.

What is the role that the parents are playing? They are being advised to give proper education to their children. This is a country rich in the tradition of giving great respect to the parents and elders. But this tradition has been well thrown to the winds. The youth of today considers them outdated, fools, clinging rigidly to their blessed ideals and not moving with times. They are made silent every time they check. They have become scared of their own children and prefer to observe perfect silence. Just give it a thought as to where we are moving today.

Perhaps, I should also think of this situation in another way. What to say of the young, the elders have also found convenient to throw all that is old and have advanced so much that life to them has the same throb as to the young ones. They are full of lust and passions, at times even more than the young and of which they are too proud. Leaving one wife for the sake of the other is a common feature of the day. On being asked "Why have you left such a devoted wife?" very quick comes the reply, "Incompatibility." Love affairs side by side the married life is the fashion of the day. What can such advanced parents teach to their own children? They allow the young all to happen under their very nose, even advise them how to go ahead in their ways.

Times are changing, I know, but that does not give permission to the society to ape the West in all its ways right or wrong. Following the West blindly has become the fashion of the day. We need to measure the pros and cons before adopting anything. Our Indian traditions are being treated with contempt. It seems to be no longer an expression of a nation's character. Our future is totally dependent upon us. Awakening to this overwhelming problem puts more pressure on us, on the individual's self-sense than on any, or on anything else ever could. A life devoted to the interests and enjoyment of the sex and lust in this world is wasted in slavery of body's desires. It may be called a dream. But with the only difference that when the dream is over, nothing is lost, but when the dream of life is over, we would have lost all.

❑

Pseudo-Spiritualism Versus Spiritualism

To understand pseudo spiritualism one needs to have a clear idea of what spirituality stands for. Spiritualism has for its base religion, not the religion of rituals and dogmas but religion that brings God and soul together. The desire to know and understand the Divine is present in all of us. To know God, men have resorted to various methods. Few are seen sitting with closed eyes meditating. Others are going about visiting sacred places trying to gain knowledge. There are those who sit in temples and other places singing hymns. Few may be roaming in forests, amongst hills and lonely places in search of the Lord. All have adopted various methods of jap, tap, fasts, reading sacred books and listening to men of knowledge. Religion helps to a great extent to arrive at a high level of living where an understanding of the Divine results in bringing about internal peace. An external lift follows which can be observed in actions that are now motivated by Love.

Spirituality requires equanimity. But we are pleasure loving people, driven by our passions, never sitting quietly to observe and understand all that is around us. We need not go far off, for the presence of the Divine is all around us. Look at the sun coming out in the morning and see it setting in the evening. Notice the birds resting in their nests at night and with the first streak of light chirping and singing. Does it make you to think what the moving force behind all this is? Does it not send a thrill within you? How cheerful the trees are as they wave their branches. Observe the blooming flowers whose very look brings within you waves of joy. Why are they so happy? They are not going to become rich, or soon would be occupying high posts. Try to learn something from them. Let us be delighted that we are also a part of the universe and one with all. Rivers flow from east and west to merge with one sea, forgetting they were ever separate. So all beings lose their separateness when they eventually merge into the Divine. You need to understand that the river that flows in others also flows in you. So all are part of the One. The result will be a feeling for all alike.

The Divine path may not be very easy but from every disappointment and defeat the spirit emerges with new strength and wider vision. On this path there is no chance of failure for it is the path of love. The desire to know God ought to be intense; intensity with sincerity, only then you can find your Lord. To know him there are no short cuts. A true incident can put my point through. It is an incident of world war II.

A French pilot by the name of Ronald Nixon was on his duty with his four colleagues when he went on flying. They had to locate the defense facilities of the German army. They soon entered the German air space, trying to hide the plane behind the skies. Nixon wanted a clear view of the defense sites. The German army was continually firing at them and it hit his plane when he was trying to bring it down to view things clearly.

Nixon was a non-believer in God and so he was never seen near the church. Observing that his plane was rapidly going down and would crash, he murmured "If there is a God, save me." He went blank after that. He lay in the hospital for two months in coma and on gaining consciousness he asked, "Where are my colleagues?" The doctors told him, "Somehow your plane re-entered the French borders and fell there. Nothing remained except you." After getting discharged from the hospital one question remained with him which haunted him day and night. "Where is he, whose name is God that has saved me. I asked Him and he has done something that was impossible. I am alive." He went about inquiring in the churches. He went to the priests and to all possible sources. He failed to get a satisfactory answer to his query. But he was very sure that he had experienced one. "But why is he not coming before me?" He was not getting an answer for this. Such thoughts possessed him and he got restless with the passing of each day. He went through Bible and other religious scripts but failed to get a satisfactory answer. Someone told him that he should go to India, a country rich on this subject of God and spirituality. He resigned from his job and came to India. He joined the Lucknow University as a teacher in English department. He did lot of reading of Upanishads, Gita, Bhagvatam and Vedas. He went about listening to great thinkers and exponents of spiritualism.

Suddenly, one day there was a flash before him and he saw one whom he was searching for. He changed his name from Nixon to Krishna Prem. God comes before those who are sincere in their search. He left this job here also and started a centre in Uttar Vrindavan. He not only saw God but was often seen talking to Him. He would speak to those who gathered every evening outside his 'muth'. He would tell them, "If I could reach Him, each one of you can also reach Him. What you require is sincerity and intensity."

One in the congregation stood up and asked, "How much sincerity and intensity?"

Krishna Prem took him by his collar and put him inside the waters of a small river running next to his place. All those gathered there were taken aback. The fellow gasped and struggled for breath. He was almost collapsing when Prem took him out and said,

"With as much intensity and sincerity with which you struggled to come out and wanted air to breath."

Spiritual gurus tell us from their experiences. We had number of gurus who rose high in the estimation of the people because of their ability. They had an impact on the audience as they were sincere guides. They had integrity. They were great thinkers. They were honest to themselves. They had no pride. Humility was their greatest asset. In them God and soul were linked together as they had complete control over their senses.

The best way to polish the heart is to remember God. We need to explore the frontiers of our consciousness. A recharging of spirit is required in which religion plays an important role. There may be different definitions given to religion, as religion is truth, religion is compassion or religion is love. But in whatever way it may be defined the essence is to know the Divine. To understand God and come close to Him is the aim of all religions. Religion in its turn becomes the base for spiritualism, for it brings about an inner resolve for an inward journey towards a higher level of thought and action and existence.

But spirituality is in no way something mysterious. It leads you to positive thinking and all spiritual thinkers are positive in nature. Spirituality and positive thinking are almost synonymous. Spiritual people possess positivity. Spiritual behaviour is like the behaviour of the rose that lives with its fragrance amidst thorns. An internal lift has lot to do with your external actions. You think divine and good actions follow. You review how the mind has worked every day. Did I cause pain to someone by my words or actions? Was my attitude aggressive? Information thus received can be transformed to knowledge on which you can base your life. It is a silent revolution where the transformation takes place in an individual soul. You can never achieve this transformation by proxy.

A pure soft mind is a gateway to Divine living. You need to soften and purify your mind. You are responsible for what you are and whatever you wish yourself to be for you have the power to make yourself. The widest possibilities for spiritual growth is to live in a spirit of give and take of every day relationships. Test of your behaviour is not how you treat the VIP's or those who matter to you but how you treat people less fortunate than you. Even if it is a little thing, do something for others, wipe out someone's tears, bring joy in the eyes of the forsaken, give hope to those who have lost all, something for which you get no pay but only the privilege of doing so. When God and soul are linked together you have within you the power to move mountains. Feel oneness with all for common good. You are the reality and when you understand this you see that you are nothing and being nothing you are everything.

This is what is spirituality. But in the modern world the concept of this spirituality which has been holding you for ages is fast losing grounds. In its place has sprung up a new ideal soon replacing the old one. A false ideology is giving way to a real one. You have a feeling that you are fast advancing due to your advancement of technology, but in a way it has resulted in only dehumanizing you.

You are fond of a life that must move on rapidly. It is so fast that you have no time to think of others. Your concern is only yourself and your well-being. You have never crossed the road to know the plight of one in trouble. You are never aware of the problems even of your next door neighbour. Sometimes you know but you are too proud to go and talk to him. You have no time to watch the lovely sunset or sunrise. You have never paused to think of the force behind all this. Divine is overshadowed by your fast paced life. You are happy to take ready-to-eat food. The bulk of your office work is somewhat completed on the mobile hanging on your chest, being used almost every minute. You are always in a deadly hurry and you cannot wait to see results. On the roads the same attitude follows. It results in traffic congestions, polluting the entire atmosphere. Noise, negativity, fast movements and cannot wait, are the features of your life.

"What is this life, if full of care

We have no time to stand and stare."

This typical life that you are leading has badly affected your attitude towards spirituality. In the place of the old and real one has sprung up a new concept of spirituality which is rightly termed as pseudo-spirituality. The craving to know the unknown is present in all of you. And this craving has given rise to religion and spirituality. But your fondness for speed and your desperate need for instant solutions has affected your attitude towards religion and spirituality. You do not have the patience to pursue the age old path to realize the Divine. But to know and understand God, there are no short cuts. At times the span of a whole life may be required. It is not so easy a path as it is made out today. You want some over-counter product that will fetch you an immediate spiritual awakening.

There is an urgent need within you to know God. You also want to be spiritualistic. Yet the ancient time tested ways are discarded as they are tedious and no longer fit for you. So as it suits the trends of the times you are satisfied embracing pseudo spirituality. Who are the ones that have to give a direction to your life. It is the 'gurus'. They are no longer the ideals of the past, who after realization have passed on the message to the people who thronged round them. Instead there have sprung up a whole lot of people, the self-styled gurus wearing costly attractive dresses to make up an appearance of a sadhu. Absolutely lacking in qualities of honesty, humility, ability, and integrity they are making a good outward show by their hair style and swinging movements. Richly dressed they are moving in the most costly cars available. With no control over their senses, the self-styled god-men are having a field day. Their show buzz attracts you and you get a strong feeling that they are 'bliss' personified. But you have to remember the age long truth that an outward appearance cannot be a reflection of the heart within. It reminds me of a great figure, Abou Hasan, the renowned spiritualist, who charmed people also by his dress and personality.

Aman came to him and said, “May I have your clothes?”. Hasan asked in surprise “Why?” Aman replied “So that in appearance at least I can look like you ‘Shanti’ personified.”

Hasan smiled and spoke softly, “Change of clothes can never change you, even if you take my skin. ‘Bhakti’ can change your heart, which is ‘tapasya’.”

Monks in monasteries, sadhus in big organizations, away from the glare of the public are carrying on activities that would put an ordinary man to shame. They are getting their bodies massaged by young ladies who had joined as devotees. They are dancing and singing and having great fun with them at night. If detected they make the excuse that they are enjoying in a similar spirit as that of Krishna with his ‘gopies’. ‘Gurus’ have been found in land grabbing cases and even secretly committing heinous crimes. Such gurus are now guiding the masses. They are exhorting you to abandon your old ways and restraints. To the seekers of spiritualism, they are ready with their easy and quick solutions. You yourself are getting attracted to such gurus because they offer you solutions that very much suit your ways and temperament. You have no control over your senses and your wandering mind. You feel greatly satisfied by the formulas that they offer you. You are told that the path of spiritualism is very easy and requires no restraints. It is soft and self-centered form of spirituality that they put before you. They totally reject the more demanding forms of beliefs. They see spirituality as a means of self-development. They want to get in touch with the inner self and with the universe but are not particularly concerned with God and His ways. Self, not selflessness, is the keynote of their spirituality.

The spiritual masters and spiritual seekers are sailing in the same boat. Today’s spiritual masters as well as seekers cannot even be remotely compared to those of the past when the guru shared with his 'shishya' his lifelong experiences. With love and understanding he taught his student. Seeker at his end received the knowledge imparted by his master with sincerity and devotion. Selflessness and divinity were the points of emphasis.

Akbar once told Tansen, "I am sure no one can sing better than you."

Tansen replied, "No, my lord, my guru sings so well that I stand nowhere near him". "Take me to him", ordered the emperor.

Tansen had to obey the orders. But on the way he was much disturbed as his guru would not sing on any one's command. What was he to do. He kept on thinking as he walked into the jungle to a renote quiet place where his guru stayed. Tansen introduced Akbar to his guru. The guru spread a mat for the king and requested him to sit down. He asked,"How is my 'shishya' doing?"

The king smiled and said, "Very well indeed." He then looked at Tansen wondering he would ask the guru to sing for him a song. Tansen in the meantime had thought of a trick to make his guru sing.

Addressing the guru, he said, "Guruji, kindly listen to this tune which you have taught me lately." Deliberately he sang in the wrong way. Immediately the guru stopped him and himself sang in the right way, showing where he went wrong. Akbar was stunned to hear him and motionless he sat there. He was in a fix for such sweetness, such melody and such vibrations he had never heard before. It sent a thrill within him. Suddenly he stood up, bowed before the guru and went out.

On the way back, he asked Tansen, "What is the secret of your guru's voice?"

Tansen replied, "My lord, I sing for you but my guru sings only for the Lord Divine. So he carries divinity in his voice, merely a reflection of which can be seen in my songs."

Dedication, love, divinity and sincerity were the threads that tied the guru to his 'shishya'.

The modern guru stands up before a huge congregation of those who wish to be his followers, raises his hands then sprinkles some water, utters few mantras, all this enough to bind them in a sacred relationship of guru and his followers. No real bindings are there to bring them together. A relationship based on flimsy grounds hardly benefits either. This is not in the spirit of the ancient texts which clearly define the role of the spiritual seeker as also the spiritual master.

In the past, India was a highly advanced spiritualistic country. Sri Aurbindo looking at the spiritual attainment of India had prophesized that India would provide spiritual leadership to the world. That India has to be a spiritual India comprising of spiritual beings united in the mission to rid the present day world of ignorance, poverty, selfishness and squalor. But where are you today? You are selfish, impatient, corrupt, false, not fit enough to stand for yourself what to say to lead the world. Instead of providing leadership you are yourself being led by the west. It is impossible now to match in any way the past spiritualism. Your fast paced environment needs bypass roads to reach to your spiritual destination. You are flagrantly throwing to the winds all the rules and laws necessary for spiritual destination. Religion no longer inculcates a spirit of sacrifice.

Sages are no longer there who gave up all for the good of others. Today spiritual guides think more for themselves, their comforts and their conveniences. Spiritual guides do not stay in hermits or in remote places. They live in palatial buildings, beautifully designed in the most modern way. Organizations come up with them. I do understand that money is required to run these organizations. But what is appalling is the hypocrisy and willful enjoyment of luxuries in the guise of sadhus and gurus. In their style of functioning, they merely cheat those whom they are expected to guide. Huge amount of money is amassed from the admirers only to be used for selfish needs.

What do you require? Not abundance of money but peace. You need to be quiet. It is essential that you soothe your nerves by no longer being hectic all the time. With a sober peaceful mind try to look within yourself. You need to go deep to realize the truth, the truth that you have divinity within you. So do all others, hence all come under one Divine. So what is your relationship with others, you will then understand. When understood your selfishness gives way to selflessness. You then begin to realize your responsibility that God had entrusted you with, namely love and service for all. When you have a calm mind, only then in silence you hear the voice of God within you. You must take off time from the hectic activities of enjoyment and selfish pursuits. Only then spiritualism grows within you.

But the pseudo guru shows you an easy path which is termed as spiritualism. "Continue to do with what you are doing and as you are doing all for yourself, there is absolutely nothing wrong in it. What you need is to do meditation. Close your eyes let your thoughts, as they are good or bad flow within you freely. Gradually try to rise above them." This is touching divinity. It sounds so attractive as it is so easy. But the question is when you close your eyes, does your silence for the while give you the calmness of mind to hear the voice of God. If not, it is only torture. Is it that your meditation gives you confidence in yourself, if not you are defeated. By your meditation do you rise up to inspire the trust of others? Not at all. So you have completely failed. But it does not matter, for if you are doing meditation, it is understood that you are very much in touch with the Divine and that is good enough to be spiritualistic. Such spiritualism is gaining ground absolutely misleading the spiritual seeker. False boundaries are being built around that are inspiring and attractive. But within there is no guarantee of spiritual growth. What you need to understand that spirituality is not about show bottle display but real transformation of heart and mind.

There are numerous spiritual guides that lull you into a way of life that makes you feel that you are living a life that is taking you near to God, but in essence you are moving further away from Divinity. A pseudo Guru in U.S. told a gathering that the new spirituality is that "You are your own best authority and as you work to know and love yourself, you discover how to live a spiritual life." The statement made by Oprah Winfrey rejects any submission to the Lord and leads you to self-justification. Selflessness is the essence of all spirituality but here there is nothing but self-justification. In modern pseudo spiritualism self gains priority.

We as a nation, has abandoned our proud heritage and rich philosophy. Spiritualism understood in the right spirit no longer guides us. We have fallen an easy prey to the West. We take pride in copying them in their style, dress, thoughts and ways of living. We are seen following their footsteps in all directions. Pseudo spiritualism is spreading like wild fire and has brought us where we are today. Well if you pray only once for a while or you close your eyes and do meditation you are in the list of the highly spiritualistic ones. America is considered as a highly spiritualistic country because 64% of its people pray. Allen Wolf of Boston college says that the spiritual searching is how to authorize the 'self' rather than God that commands. It is about finding a religion that gives 'you' all the powers and make 'self' all important. The result of all this has led us to what Earnest Gains asks:

"Why is it that, as a culture, we are more comfortable seeing two men holding guns than holding hands?"

Your mad rush to copy the West has only resulted in bringing you down. A sage showed lamp when it was bright sunshine. When asked why he was doing like that he replied:

"Even then you cannot see yourself. Madly you are following others, without using your brains. You cannot see your very self. I am trying to show that to you".

You need a sage to show you where you are running. Technical advancement does not mean advancement in the real sense. Technology and wealth without inner wisdom and devotion are nothing. Technology is still a toddler and yet it makes tall claims. It believes that finally it will surpass cosmic laws. Technology has destroyed transcendence from our reality map with no concern about the existence of a higher reality, the one that has no beginning or end. It is resulting finally in giving "SELF" all importance which is bringing you down spiritually. Wake up then before it gets too late.

Imitating others you have taken to ways that have brought you to spiritual bankruptcy. India has a rich heritage and has always been considered as one leading in spiritualism. Spiritualism in India is older than history, older than tradition and even older than legend and looks twice as old as all put together. Something so deeply embedded cannot be so easily rooted out. Lack of trust in spiritual goodness is the cause of corruption today, which has gone so widespread here and has brought you down.

Since you alone are responsible for your ways and thoughts, you alone can change things. Sooner than later you will realize that you have gone astray from the straight, strong, good path into the muddy, marshy, dirty side lane where your feet have got stuck up in the mud. You need only to learn the principles of right living. You have only to change the character of your action from selfishness to selfless service. Mend the quality of your emotion from preferential attachment to universal love. Raise your knowledge from the mundane to the Supreme Self within. Times will not be far off when the entire prevailing atmosphere will change. I have no doubts that your hunger for love and for the Divine will bring you to your old, gold ways of spiritualism and Bhagvat Geeta. The concept of the West that 'Self', 'glitter'. 'technology' and 'wealth' are great will soon lose its sheen and in its place will rise up an India strong with its spiritual values. The West need not consider you as fools or weak for you have a potential that goes much above them, you have the spiritual strength.

❑

In-Laws

Past times tell us of hardships that a bride had to face as she entered the house of her husband and her in-laws. The daughters-in-law have struggled hard. Harsh words, abuses, and ill treatment that they met are heart-breaking. As a daughter she got lot of love and care from her father and mother. The shift from this atmosphere of peace and care to that of responsibilities, rebukes and scolding, was a scenario that left her absolutely paralyzed. A little repose she got at times was from her husband. Or perhaps from some other relation, sympathetic towards her, who happened to be living with them. But they went through their lives quietly. Many times they found refuge in prayers and devotion to God. They were found persevering and lead a life that became hard and pitiable. Much can be argued in their favour and against the parents-in-law.

But things do not go on forever in the same way and later if not sooner the daughters-in-law found opportunities and revolted against a life that they found was disgusting.They felt enough was enough and they need to have their own way. A violent change has taken place in society which has shattered the quietness of the in-laws, who are now told in clear words by the daughters-in-law that they need to attune their minds and hearts to their vibrations, else they should be ready to face the worst. The parents-in-law are now fishing in cold waters and need the same sympathy that was once given to the young brides as they entered their new homes of the in-laws. The situations now are embarrassing and leave a severe dent on the young and a strong resentment on the part of the old. With love, care and immense sacrifices parents bring up their sons. It is rightly said that when one decides to make a child, one should be ready to see the heart walk outside the body. They are overjoyed when he gets a good job. In all this they seem to realize that their dreams had come true. But their aspirations do not end here. They look for a bride that would give them good company, afford them rest, give support to their failing strength and brighten their loneliness with sounds of laughter. Sounds that would be louder as the little ones would make their appearances.

Dream driven with enthusiasm and hopes of great joy they welcome the new guest, the bride, as she enters the home to become a part of their lives. Amidst sounds of joy and music the mother-in-law does 'arti' as she shows this new comer the way to enter her home and into her life. What happens then?

Misunderstandings and heart-breaking situations? Is it the lack of mutual trust between the young and the old that brings the crash? Or is it the generation gap that creates the problem? Why there is an utter lack of considerations? What ails their understanding? These need to be studied.

In a survey conducted recently and reported in a reputed daily newspaper "Times of India" about the senior citizens and their percentages on different sources of grievances it was pointed out that 60% of them were harassed by their sons and various percentages were given on many various such headings. But when the percentage came to the issue of being tormented by their daughters-in-law, it was 100%. Not one out of all the vast numbers interviewed spoke in favour of his daughter-in-law. Such is the grand reputation that they enjoy today.

A father gave the name Shravan Kumar to his notorious son. It is a name well known of a son whose whole life was dedicated to the service of his parents. A neighbour asked the father, "Why have you given this name to your son when he does not have a single quality of Shravan Kumar. In fact he violates every norm of a dutiful son."

The father replied, "My son has a great quality very similar to Shravan."

The neighbour was quite surprised and asked him "Please do mention even one such quality in your son, and I bet I will give you a hundred rupee note."

The father smiled and said, "He considers his parents blind."

It is a thought provoking reply that well states the view of the growing sons about their parents in the present age.

The daughter-in-law enters her new home and soon finds that all is not to her taste. She tells her partner, "The house is so ill managed that it makes me sick to live here."

"Go ahead and rearrange as you wish", the husband lovingly replies. She goes and tells the parents, "This room that you are occupying is the central room." "Yes" the mother rejoins, "it is for safety that we are sitting here."

"We have to meet visitors as they would come here", was the prompt reply "and official visitors would not like to meet you. Moreover my people and friends would feel too bad if you interfere", said the daughter-in-law with disdain.

"So what is to be done?" the father asked.

"Please move to the back corner of the house and let me change this room into a drawing room", replied the daughter-in-law.

"Well, we can then shift to the side room", replied the mother-in-law.

"Oh no! that will be our bed room. You have to go to the back corner room", insisted the daughter-in-law.

"But have you asked my son?" came a weak voice of a depressed mother.

"It is he who has asked me to do it" was a curt reply.

The parents quietly agreed and shifted to the back corner of the house. The mother felt too bad and complained to her husband "Is it the first welcome signal that is given to us?"

The father was quiet and after some time he said "All that we have to do is to go off to that corner, for that is the place that rightly belongs to us in their lives. A corner fit for servants only."

The old and the young have lost the harmony that ought to have prevailed between them. But why?

The pin pricks are given every other day. These cause pain that exceeds the most severe pains. "Do not touch this as it is very expensive. You will spoil it", orders the daughter-in-law. "My husband has bought it for me." "Did you pick up my locket that I left on my table" asked the daughter-in-law. Tears rolled down from the eyes of the mother-in-law as she lamented "Am I a thief in my own house?"

As the father-in-law was taking out a bottle of campa from the fridge, the daughter-in-law shouted from the back "Papa it becomes very expensive for us as you consume two bottles per day. We keep this only for guests."

"I will be careful" came the quiet reply, as the father hung his head and walked off quietly.

"You never inform us when you go out" asked the mother.

"We are now grown-ups and need not inform you where and when we go", replied the son rudely. The mother was stunned and was left wondering whether he was the same son that she had brought up with so much care and love.

Such pin pricks continue and gradually become worse. "The servants do not listen to us", complained the mother.

"Just leave them. If they run away who is going to do the work?" replied the son unconcerned.

"As it is you who do no work, only sit and talk", joined the daughter-in-law.

Yes, they understood the lesson which they took long to understand.

A son, Arjun, after a week, when the bride joined the family of the in-laws, came and told the father, something that almost broke his heart.

"Papa, you have put this house in my name, as it is rightly called "Arjun Bhawan". I have planned to sell it off and buy some modern style flat in some posh colony".

"In a house that you have lived so happily and with so much pride for twenty-five years you find within seven days of your wife joining you as worthless and unfit. You were so slow in learning lessons when I taught you but I must congratulate you that there is someone who can teach you lessons in no time", sarcastically replied the father.

The son was quiet for some time and then said, "So can Igo ahead with my plan?"

"My dear son, I have laboured hard to save throughout my service and then constructed this house. You will do well to do the same. I was careful to put my name on the papers and not yours observing the wind that is blowing in the present world" replied the father thoughtfully. The daughter-in-law was very sad to hear this. She immediately decided to leave the old alone and live with her husband in a rented flat in a posh colony where she enjoyed her ways and was happy.

The two, the mother and the father are together to sympathize with each other in their agony. They reconcile to their bad luck and life somehow flows on. But the situation worsens when the mother is unfortunate to face all the hardships alone. It becomes difficult to bear the brunt. She is crushed down completely in her loneliness. An old mother, poor thing, was abused so much by the daughter-in-law that she would be deeply hurt, but what brought tears in her eyes was when her own son well tutored by his clever wife joined her in her cutting remarks against his own mother. She would then run off to some neighbour and pass the night there. By morning when she became quiet, she would come back home. The practice continued for some time but not for long. She did not return one day. The son thought she was playing some trick and did not bother for her. But when she failed to make her appearance for three consecutive days, he got worried and started looking for her. He went to the neighbours to enquire about her but was told that she was not with them. He went about all possible places to search her. He even went to an astrologer, who happened to be my husband, to ask as to when she would come back. When finally one day, after an interval of three days, on the newspaper information that a body was found floating on the waters of Jumna and needed identification, he ran to identify it, and found it was none but her sweet mother who spoke to him in her dead silence quietly yet sweetly.

"I bless you my child, I waited for you here but you got a little late." The son broke down as he embraced the dead body of his mother. But why then he was abusing her? Why then he listened to the coated stories of his wife? Why did he begin to cut her very soul by his words and actions? Why? Who is to answer?

The mother did answer in her quietness, "If both of you could have just put your thoughts and minds together positively and come across to me, we would have held our hands together and watched the rising sun. But first have you ever experienced my pain? Well, you have to wait till you too go through it."

The son is responsible in many ways for the present condition that largely prevails in society. He becomes so weak after marriage that he completely surrenders himself to his wife blindly forgetting all his considerations elsewhere. If she says in the night, it is day, it becomes a day for him and he sees the sun shining and if she says during the day it is night the day changes accordingly. He begins to accept all without reservations, without probing into the propriety of things and without hesitation. A father too proud of his son on observing the plight of other parents would too often boast, "At least my son would never change." Tragedy overtook him when within a month after marrying his son he was spotted sitting with a swollen face. When asked "What is the matter that you are so sad?"

He merely replied, "My son is no longer my son."

The parents suffer not so much from the behaviour of their daughters-in-law, but from the fast changing attitude of their sons.

The daughter-in-law enters from outside and may not have much sympathies for the in-laws, but a son who loved the parents should go against them is the pain that hurts them badly. It is something that is seen happening all round. Do we call this a shift to modernity: Does being modern mean that we leave all that is good in our traditions, as old and therefore worthless? There are exceptions everywhere, though their number may be very small and surprising. It is a true incident of five brothers who lived happily with their parents. The eldest got married and the first thing he did was to leave the lot and move out under the wise advice of his wife. The second did the same and the third and the fourth acted in the similar manner, all under the wise guidance of their wives. Then came the turn of the fifth. The wife looked around and told her husband "Why your old father who is incapable of doing any work and this old mother be our responsibility? They should be asked to go away."

"But where will they go. In fact, I may tell you that this entire building in which all of us are living belongs to them", the husband replied.

"Others do not care for them why should we?" asked an irritated wife.

"If others are wrong it does not follow that we should also do the same. They love me so much" entreated the husband "and they have no one to care for them."

"I do not care, please ask them to pack up and sit at any other place they want to" replied the disgusted wife.

"In that case you can pack up your things and go to the place from where you have come. I need someone who can look after them" the husband answered quietly.

The wife got a clear message and accordingly adjusted herself and for long she lived happily with them.

If seriously analyzed, we can see that the daughters-in-law may not be blamed so much as your very sons who are ready to join hands with them. A daughter-in-law may not have good feeling for the parents-in-law. But what about the son? He has loved and lived with them for long. Why should they become hostile? And that too on the suggestions of his wife. Why should they lose their balance and good sense. The mothers-in-law are well advised to treat their daughters-in-law as their own daughters but a pertinent question arises from their side, as to why they should not treat them as their own mothers. If that was so it was an ideal situation with all problems solved. Instead it has become a common phenomena of our society that the economically independent parents quietly walk out of their homes and live a quiet independent, peaceful life outside. If there are two, the father and the mother-in-law, they hold hands in sympathy and walk out to join some old home which are being overflooded these days. The real tragedy is with those who are old, economically weak, who must live tight lipped in some remote corner of the house dancing at the whims of the daughters-in-law.

What we need today is to reach towards a harmony that must prevail and is essential for the good of society. This needs our urgent attention. What is this life about if our own connections remain superficial and we fail to arrive at any solution? Both sides need to come together, the older ones by its experience and knowledge and the younger ones by its respect and considerations. It is only after proper balancing that we can hope for better results.

The relations so far have been dark enough. But it is time that we can see the stars.

We have to create a climate in which our differences, our grievances with one another must not prevent us from coming together and engaging ourselves in a meaningful dialogue and work together for an acceptable solution. Today's world calls for partnerships and alliances all round, why then we should break amongst our very own? We have to move forward from self-centered existence to co-existence. Let us then move from confrontation to interaction. We need collaboration and not alienation. To achieve this we need a common understanding from both sides. I think it will be wrong to feel that we can remain aloof. We must try to overcome our differences by meaningful dialogues where both parties should come together, bring up their problems, and have open discussions, hiding nothing from each other, all trying to give due considerations to each other and then arriving to conclusions that would make it possible for all to live a life where there is perfect understanding from all sides. Transparency will greatly work in coming to some right solutions. There ought to be no talking behind the back, no more false accusations, but trying to get into an atmosphere of peace and happiness for both sides.

Let us at least draw some inspiration from the children who never hold grudges. They fight when they play together, but they quickly make up and laugh and continue to play. Their fights never deteriorate into bitter feuds. Why then the grown-ups are becoming worse? Why their intelligence is going waste? It is time for all to wake up.

❑

Surgery in Hospitals

In any operation the two that are important are the surgeon and the anesthetic. If one is missing the operation cannot be performed. The success or the failure of an operation depends on the COMPETENCE OF BOTH. So they walk together hand in hand while accomplishing the task that they have before them. With the skill of a surgeon, the anesthetic needs to perform intelligently if any operation has to be successful. I know of only one case where a very famous doctor lost his job in a government hospital in Lucknow because of the wrong assessment of an anesthetic. He administered an overdose of anesthesia. He could not bring the patient to consciousness after the operation and the patient died. He lost his job with the doctor. In all cases the intelligence of the anesthetic works towards the success of the surgeon in his operation. But who cares for him in his wonderful work he otherwise performs?

An operation becomes successful, the surgeon is applauded, but has anyone gone to praise the anesthetist for the good job that he has done? No one knows the great task that he too had performed. The situation is like that of a boy who is scolded and punished for his bad show but when he goes par excellence, there is no one to pat his back. Is it not injustice? It is enough to pull down his morale. It dawns upon him a feeling that why at all he should do hard work. He should pass away his time casually and with ease. It is this psychology that seems to work with the anesthetist. He is paid for his job. So let him do his work comfortably, never taking risks and never going beyond his time, five o'clock sharp. He must wind off his work and be at home to enjoy the company of his wife and children.

I think most of us, deep in our worldly ways will smile and say mischievously, "Why what is wrong in his thinking, it is quite natural, he is amply justified." The surgeons point their fingers on anesthetists for lack of enthusiasm and lack of taking initiative. We need not give heed to them. But let us analyse the entire situation and see why at all the surgeons and the anesthetists are at loggerhead. Who is wrong? Who is right? Who is to be condemned? Does life mean only superficial appearances, or does it have a deeper meaning attached to it. Does life mean walking only on a sure and smooth ground, or it means crossing the hurdles that might come on the way to reach a required destination. To me life appears to be a struggle, a struggle to do good to others, to save them from pain and sufferings. It means trying without giving up or giving in. It means doing one's best in anything one is chosen to do. And when the goal is sacred, so sacred as to save lives, one needs to achieve it through commitment and hard work.

Old age in itself is a great problem. But many added problems come up to increase its trouble. Purushottam was given a kick by his brother, when he fell down and broke his hip bone. Already suffering from mental pain, his physical pain added to his worry. He went to the doctor in the hospital who told him that he needed an immediate surgery. The patient readily agreed for anything that would lessen his pain and was admitted in the hospital. But the surgeon could perform the surgery if he got a nod from the anesthetist. Purshottam, it was found had high blood pressure. So he could not get the signal from the anesthetist right out. A physician was consulted who put Purushottam on the drugs to bring down his blood pressure. After a week on the drugs, the blood pressure came to normal range except for occasional readings where it was 5-6 mm more than the desired readings. The physician was satisfied with the outcome of his drugs and did not want any further change in the medication. Purushottam was taken to the operation theatre but returned from there since the anesthetist was still not satisfied with the control of Purushotam's blood pressure and wanted at least 10 days of consistent blood pressure readings absolutely within the normal range. The surgeon requested the anesthetist, "I think you can take a little risk, so that I can perform the operation. Going back from the operation theatre three times itself is good enough for his blood pressure to shoot up. You know with the passing of time his condition is taking a serious turn. He may be in a suboptimal status but will never become better than what he is today. Continuously lying on the bed, at an age of seventy years, he has started developing bedsores and cough too. Today it is marginally raised blood pressure but tomorrow he is going to be loaded with infection of the lungs, bed sores and may be with the urine infection too." "Oh no, Sir" responded the anesthetist, "Why should I take risk and put myself in trouble. Am I paid for the risks? You will not side me if something goes wrong." It made the surgeon feel sorry for the patient but he was helpless.

Who is to be blamed? The surgeon for not insisting strongly? Or the anesthetist for keeping his obstinate stand? It is for you to decide. The patient died. Perhaps the anesthetist could have saved his life, only if he had some feeling for a person who was like a father to him. A calculated risk should not have been a problem with him. An anesthetist stands as a savior, though invisible but with a role as powerful as of God. One would ask the anesthetist if only he could have behaved with the dignity of the role assigned to him!

Nandu was to be operated for his hernia problem. Already for the day, the anesthetist had done three cases, but if he took up the fourth, it would make him to sit and inonitor the case beyond his dead-mark five o'clock. He comes and tells the surgeon, "Nandu cannot be operated". "Why?" surgeon asked in surprise "still there is so much of time". "Time is no problem, Sir," though that was his real problem. Trying to feign very concerned and honest, he tells the surgeon “I saw Nandu smoking as I entered the hospital in the morning and you know tobacco will create havoc if anesthesia is administered.” The surgeon called the patient who on oath said, “What of today, I have not smoked for a fortnight as directed.” But the anesthetist had to believe his eyes and not any oath. He had some important appointment and he knew well that if he took Nandu’s case he would get late, so he made an excuse to honour his appointment. See the irony of the situation as to who gets the preference!

The anesthetist has many excuses ready to be used, suiting the occasion. Excuses are often made up than real. Surgeons do keep some reserve patients in the operation list so that even if few patients get unfit for anesthesia for various unforeseen reasons, the operating time and the theatre facilities would remain utilized by those in the reserve list. It may cause the patients hardships like remain on fast and wait for the whole day for their turn to come but despite this, it is quite usual to find the whole operation list together with its reserve list collapsing for want of so called proper preoperative anesthetic fitness of the patients.

“No.1. patient Durga Das cannot be operated.” ‘Why?” asks the surgeon. “This is going to be a long time surgery and that too around the spinal cord. I feel, after the operation table, he may require a bed in the intensive care ward, and I have no bed free in my ICU. So he cannot be operated today.” “Bring in the next, it is Rahim, so bring him in, the doctor requests. “Well Sir, he too cannot be operated.” The surgeon is surprised “Reason?” “Blood pressure is his problem”, replies the anesthetist. The doctor says, “I have taken his blood pressure an hour back and found it quite normal.” “My instrument tells otherwise and I can believe my instrument only.” The surgeon in despair calls for the next. It is Prem. Again the anesthetist informs him “Well, he has a patch in his left lung. We wanted the three consecutive sputum’s report which is not available, so he cannot be brought to your table.”

The surgeon annoyed argues, "But the patient does not have the slightest cough. Where will he bring out the sputum from? Physician has opined it to be an old healed patch. We have already given him the five days course of antibiotic also" but all in vain did the surgeon argue.

Therefore, for the whole day, no patient could be operated, be it the surgical team's inability or the patient's destiny for not conforming with the preoperative standards of the anesthetic team. Calculate the colossal waste of money that was incurred in the payment of the salary to the surgeon, the anesthetist and the entire team of the nurses, theatre assistants and attendants, besides the cost of the theatre space and the expensive equipment. It makes a big dent on the public purse that is given to the hospitals. Any suboptimal fitness of the patient could endanger his life will be the standard and the formidable answer from any anesthetist. But are they justified in behaving in a manner which may theoretically be the perfect way but smells of cheat and callousness towards human lives and sufferings. The self-defense often amounts to deceit.

I may well narrate an incident here that happened in the life of my father. It made him to suffer but has made me to think seriously. A very renowned surgeon, known for his good surgical hand, in a famous government hospital advised my father for some endoscopic surgery. My father was discovered to have mild rise in his blood pressure and the border line diabetes too. I ran from pillar to post for nearly two weeks and exhausted my patience chasing neurologist to orthopedic surgeons in a futile attempt to get preanasthetic clearance. My father had to undergo MRI of the back for his occasional sciatica kind of back pain and a CT scan of the brain since he had disclosed a spell of mild giddiness 2-3 months ago. Undergoing the drill of such extensive encounters with so many specialist and so many procedures, my father failed to maintain the blood pressure strictly within the range of 130/80 mm Hg. It occasionally climbed to 134 and 84 and thus was not entitled for strict absolute fitness for anesthesia for the elective surgery. Waiting thus for arriving at the perfect condition as thought by the anesthetic, my father got disgusted and we went over to a private hospital and that very day he was successfully operated. He was happy that he was relieved of his pain but unhappy that the services of a very good surgeon in a government hospital were denied to him and also the heavy amount that he had to pay in the private hospital.

In my mind there arose a volley of questions. Why the anesthetist in the government hospital refused while the anesthetist in the private hospital did not make any fuss about it? Is it the lack of experience? Is it the sense of complacency that one develops in government jobs? Is it the job security that does not allow him to take risks and move forward? Is it the lack of courage and honesty? What is it on the part of the anesthetist that gives him a callous attitude towards the patient? Or is it the disparity in the payment made in the public and private hospitals? What is it? A large junk of human population in India can only afford government hospitals. They look to the doctors and surgeons here. If the anesthetist is unhappy for any reason whatsoever why is he targeting the poor and the helpless? Why is it that he is killing his own conscience? Why is he concerned only about his own selfish needs? Why is it that he adopts an attitude of non-cooperation with the surgeon? Why? I fail to understand. If he is paid less, he should target the right place. Why his aim is always the poor patient?

I do not wish to conclude that the anesthetist should not act with responsibility trusted to him. All that he needs is courage and confidence and honesty to achieve his goal. He is like a magician who waves his magic wand and the patient closes his eyes. He then goes on and repeats the process to make him awake and aware. With love, and with responsibility, if he does what he will, there is no risk and there is no conflict. Also let not anesthetist be confined to his own personal comforts. Let him build up in himself the courage to draw new ways to act with responsibility to help the ailing. Cultivating a close feeling for the patient and trying to co-operate with the surgeon in a positive way, he will remove whatever fears or insecurities he may have. It will give him the strength to cope with obstacles that he may encounter.

However we may push up the surgeon, it is the anesthetist that plays a very vital role. He may be invisible to the patient or to those around him, but without his services no operation can take place. I met a surgeon who told me that in some of the cases, it is the brilliancy of an anesthetist that plays a more vital role than that of the surgeon. For example in an open heart surgery, a surgeon ties the vessels which are as easy as tying vessels elsewhere in the body but it is on the brilliancy and competence of the anesthetist that the success of the operation depends. The surgeon knows well that it is the firm hand of an anesthetist that holds him firmly.

Twins were born, but they were joined together. They were successfully separated by the surgeon but the controlling power of life was in the hands of an anesthetist. For the first time, I read in the paper, what must have been the common story, "The work of the anesthetist needs to be commended as the operation lasted for thirty six hours."

A renowned heart surgeon was compelled to leave the hospital in which he was working for long. He joined another hospital, but he made it clear to the authorities that he would join only on the condition that his anesthetist with his team would also come with him. He knew well the value of the co-operation of the anesthetist. A close co-operation was the seed to his success and progress. Moving together at every step was the confidence and courage of the doctor surgeon.

I am not trying to give a clean chit to a surgeon and throw out the anesthetist into the mud. I only wish to insist upon a harmony that is needed between the two. Overlooking one's individual gain or loss and moving towards a destination that lifts up the society ought to be their goal. What I ask for is the strength, courage and co-operation that ought to be the moving force behind all their actions. They have opportunities that they must seize. Situations may be impossible, as they are in the medical world, but it is their putting their heads together that can do wonders. There is no situation that is not transformable; they can turn the worst into best. The decision is entirely theirs. They are the ones that are faced with a series of great opportunities, brilliantly disguised as impossible situations. Seize common occasions and make them great. We are still looking hopefully towards you both.

Both the surgeon as well as the anesthetist have a sacred task to perform. They are equally great in their own fields. Their aim should be to go in a way where they widen their circle of compassion to embrace all the living. If they have to achieve anything, both will walk hand in hand smiling, and never shirking from doing real service to mankind. The brilliance of the anethetist may go unrecognized by his fellow men. But his conscience will lift him up. Remember, my dear anesthetist, your reward will come from the Divine from whom nothing goes unseen.

❑

My Visit to Amarnath

My father would often tell me, when I was a child, about different places that are considered sacred and need to be visited if one has time, opportunity, strength and faith. In the North Badrinath and Kedarnath. In the South, Mahabaleshwar. In the East, Jaganathpuri and in the west Dwarkadhish. It gave one a sense of unity in diversity. One also gets acquainted with different types of men with different tastes and with different views. It was all so very interesting to hear him. But when my father would come to Amarnath, he would close his eyes with reverence and say, "Oh! this is a place impossible to reach. Great height and that so very steep that one can only imagine and say "Om Namah Shivai" and leave it there.

I always wondered in my dreams if I could ever reach Amarnath. As times passed I was happy to visit all these places that my father had mentioned. Yet deep inside there stood within me a craving, an intense desire to have Amarnath's darshan, about which I was continually hearing stories. It did disturb me at times and I wished I could come up to the impossible.

Life went on and it so happened that I became a great devotee of Ma Durga. With Her I came close to Lord Shiv also. Hurdles in my life were too many, at times difficult to cross, almost defeating me. Once I was pulled down so badly that I lost faith in my deep faith. Misfortunes after mistunes hit me so badly that I stood lost. I was like a ship that was caught in the storm with no one to steer it out. In such a state I found strength in holding Her hand. She pulled me out, though for some time I was too annoyed with Her for giving me so much of misery despite my devotion to Her. Caught in the storm of utter despair and isolation, I came back to Her, for I felt that She had at least some feelings for me. My scorn for Her gave way which changed my very life. Now it is Her strength, that pilots me and Her words that direct me. Once again I am at Her feet with love and affection. I find great repose over here and any problem that I face I bring it to Her. I had no one so close to me so I got into the bad habit of troubling Her too often. But I always found Her smiling. My devotion to Her has deepened and I find real joy in visiting Her shrines and offering prayers to Her. She has become a part of myself and I am never without a thought of Her.

After retirement, my life became passive, positively inactive but I felt a great relaxation in it. Life as it is happening now, I began to appreciate and rejoice in it. It gave me time to move out frequently to my visits to various shrines. But every time I wished to visit the temple of Lord Shiva, obstacles would come in my way and I was denied His darshan. Despite my intense desire, I could never reach Him. I took this problem to my Ma, as my practice was and asked Her "Is Lord Shiva angry with me? He is never allowing me to come to Him." A strange event took place which made me sure that Lord Shiva was not happy with me. A shivling which I had kept with reverence disappeared from my puja room. Every day I gave bath and applied chandan on it. I looked round and searched for it everywhere, but it was not to be found anywhere. My heart sank, for one thing I had kept with great care had disappeared with suddenness. It was with me for the last thirty years. But now with a special seat meant only for Him and puja room always closed carefully, it had disappeared mysteriously. It shook my heart and I was sure that all was not going to be well. Lord Shiva being annoyed with me, had left me and the worst is to follow. I had my apprehensions to the full.

As the practice was, I took the problem to my Ma. In answer I got a call from Lord Kaleshwar, and I did not lose time in responding to it. I got ready and ran fast to catch this precious opportunity. Soon I was at Kaleshwar temple. Winters were on but I got ready for morning darshan. I took bath at 2o'clock, in the bleak darkness of the night. I shivered as I came out of my room. But there was warmth in the feelings that I was going to meet Lord Shiva. Certain norms had to be followed. Sari is a must and no woolens can be worn. I was fortunate enough to get my chance of pouring milk mixed with water on the Shivling. I came out and sat on the ground before it, folding my hands and closing my eyes. Vibrations sweet and strong ran within me that shook my whole body. I felt strange sensations and prayed, "My Lord, I hope you are no longer angry with me. I felt so when you had disappeared with suddenness from my pooja room. Forgive me for whatever wrong I might have committed in my thoughts or in my actions."

I stepped out of the temple into the market outside and I saw the same type of shivling that I had lost. I refused to buy one and resisted all such feelings, for I did not wish to suffer in agony that I had gone through once. Fears and disappointments were too many in my life und I did not wish to add to the numbers. I stayed for three days and I visited market many times but I kept myself away successfully from the temptation of buying a shivling again. On the last day, I got a call from my daughter requesting me to buy a shivling for her. I went to buy one for her but the other jumped in to occupy its place in my pooja room. How and why I cannot answer.

Perhaps this was not enough. With a strange suddenness, for which I fail to account, there rose within me a strong desire to visit Amarnath. I had always considered it an impossibility, something I should never entertain. I had left it and was satisfied. But at this time it came with a force too strong to resist. I felt odd but it impelled me to go ahead. Who was moving me like that? I did not know, but some divine power I was sure. The feeling took a strong hold on me and I was willing to face all odds that came in my way. At any cost I was willing to move ahead. I was ready to move ahead at the cost of dangers, at the cost of inconveniences and at the cost of annoying my son, who so much cares for me. All efforts were made to dissuade me, but nothing could stop me. I moved forward. Within me was a strong feeling that I will get the darshan as some divine power was pulling me towards it. It was all very strange to account for. It would be a dream come true. Even the thought of death in facing all types of odds did not deter me for I agreed with Socrates who talked about death as, "the greatest blessing of all human blessings."

Nothing is impossible if the call is coming from above. Some power was taking me to the path, wherein my father would say, "close your eyes and say namaskar to Amarnath, where only the few selected would reach." Was I among the selected few at the moment? Yes it looked so. Despite numerous problems that confronted me I was ready to go ahead. An urge from within, a determination to succeed in my mission and a feeling that some power was protecting me gave me a sense of surety that nothing would go amiss.

I am really bad at any future planning. In fact I do not do any planning at all. I never think of what I am doing tomorrow. I do not maintain a diary. Things come up and I accept them. After much discussion and debate we, my son, my daughter and an attendant landed on the plane which brought us to Srinagar. We took a taxi and immediately started for Baltal. This journey was very tedious for oft and on we had to wait for long to get any indication to go ahead. The police refused to give signals for the car to move on. We stood for hours in the crowded jams. It was getting dark, it was continually raining and it was very cold. All were scolding me for the venture that was taken because of me. I was quiet. Somehow after a very tiring journey we landed at Baltal.

Here at Baltal a hut was reserved for us. It was no romantic shelter as you are inclined to imagine but a dungeon with no facilities at all. Few essential services were provided but in a horrible way. The iron bed shook violently as I tried to lie down on it. No proper bedding was available. I shivered in the bitter cold. All woolens that I had carried I put on myself but it was insufficient to keep the cold away. Darkness accompanied by cold and a continuous drizzle made the entire atmosphere bleak and unpleasant. I had arrived at Srinagar comfortably and the forward path from Baltal looked easy. But in between there was so much of harassment that it made me very nervous. Perhaps it was all to make me understand that the divine path is really not easy. It requires lot of courage to face both mental and physical tensions apart from possessing a deep faith. I stood on the door of the hut to have a view of the outside. I was surprised to see so many sitting under the shelter of the trees or under the torn umbrellas. They had only plain sheets to cover them. I felt quite uneasy to see them. Was it their faith that stood behind then to give them strength? Perhaps yes. I stood nowhere near them in their faith. I may not have been in the best of conditions but I was definitely in a much better and a comfortable situation than theirs. Certainly their faith had deepened. Faith I felt is an experience, an insight and an intuition which takes its own time to come. I saluted their faith which gave them the strength to face the worse. My troubles dwindled before theirs and I stood fast for their spirit infused within me the power to face the most difficult situation. It brought a smile on my face for I got a good clue from them. I came in and instead of thinking about cold, I turned my thoughts to my Mother Divine. I took out my mala and started my jap, trying hard to concentrate on the divine. When nothing seems to help and I am in utter despair, Her thoughts always bring relief. I went off to sleep and got up in the morning, waking others to get ready for our onward march. The drizzle outside continued but with the dawn came the warmth and a message that with reverence we must start. As time went on the weather became softer and more friendly. The drizzle stopped and the sun could be seen coming out. Was my Mother Divine taking care of me? Was She so much concerned about me? It looked so.

We soon reached the place from where the helicopter started, and waited patiently for our turn. The few minutes that I spent sitting in the helicopter were wonderful. From above I realized the vastness of the universe and the all-pervading power. I felt that the same pervading power that runs through my veins night and day runs through the world of nature and dances in rhythmic measure covering it. Huge mountains stood with grandeur, with the growth of tall trees and glaciers moved amongst them. And when my eyes looked down searching for the place where they stood I could see streams running at the base, singing the lovely tune, "For men may come and men may go, but I go on forever." It was wonderful. There burst within me an explosive inner light, more brilliant and more powerful than the sun. It symbolized the light of the divine. As this grace light empowered me, my heart and my mind was lighted up with the divine radiance and intelligence. It kindled within me a strange feeling of oneness with all. This light brought a new type of consciousness beyond logic, of the flowering of the heart centre. I was stunned to see all around me such grandeur, such majesty with which nature stood. A strange feeling stirred my heart, a feeling of unity with the divine. I sat motionless absorbed in my thoughts and feelings. A strong jerk with which the helicopter landed on the ground woke me up and brought me out to myself and I got up to come down.

I was put in a palaki, to be carried by two men. I hated such a position, but with my broken knees I had to accept it. I could not climb those hundred stairs that took me up to get a glimpse of the divine. I had so much of strength once but Her blessings were missing. Today when the heart weeps for what I have lost, my spirit laughs for what it has gained. So what if I am old, I am eighty today, I have no feeling that I have ceased to grow. Because I am growing inwardly. What I am concerned is the readiness with which I must obey my Mother Divine, Her call for love and forgiveness. I sat in the palaki and looked and I saw the vast surge of humanity, all moving up with faces that had brightened up with hopes and faith. The grace light kindled within me. It brought an awareness within me of my being a part of them.

Not only that but a strong feeling of oneness, of compassion and of love for others and for all. It moved me from self-absorbed and self-centered perspective to an experience of inter connectedness and universal oneness. Here was present the great cosmic energy of which I had read at many places that has the power to change our very lives. The mystery of grace I do not understand, but definitely it moves me on.

On I went till I was brought down from the palaki leaving for me a few steps to go up. I climbed those steps and saw before me a huge tall shivling, absolutely white as it was of snow. The snow fell from the cave, but what was surprising, it fell so naturally as to form a perfect shape of a shivling. It was fifteen feet in height. I had to move back and raise my head to see the shivling. An aura of mystery surrounded it. It was a figure sublime, that stood with majesty. My hands came together to be folded and my head bent down in reverence. I stood in silence and stunned as tears rolled down my cheeks in sheer joy. The place vibrated with positive energy and for a while I felt I was in heavens.

I was allowed to stand there for ten minutes, a favour not allowed to others. An aura of peace pervaded the place and I felt within myself an energy that shook my whole body.

Yes, sages have rightly said that once upon a time Lord Shiva sat here to talk to his wife, Parvati. I felt their presence even now. My mind rose high, my heart throbbed and my very soul stirred within me. The joy and the thrill I felt was unparalleled which no amount of riches could have afforded me. Even the cave under which shivling stood was very high and inspiring. The mountain was of the colour, I would say off-white. It had streaks of brown lines on it. From below the colour gave an impression, to an onlooker that it is all snow, but from near, I could see that even without snow, it gave that impression. The mountain well enhanced the grandeur of the place. As I closed my eyes, I remembered my father's words, "Close your eyes, bow down, think of Him, and forget that you can ever reach there." Today it was very different.

With the blessings of my Ma Divine, a dream had come true. I am sure my father watching me from the heavens would have been be too pleased to see me there, standing before Amarnath. The very thought of Lord Shiva exalted my being, brought light to my heart, life to my soul and my whole being exulted. I stood motionless offering my prayers to my Lord,

"If You had disappeared from my pooja room, it was to bring me close to Yourself. Certain You were not angry with me. Yet I am too scared of Your anger. I need Your blessings, this would inspire me with right thoughts and which would give a right direction to my life. Only You can help me to learn that I must count on my blessings, for life is always so unfair." So saying, I was silent for some time to feel the great presence of the almighty. A violent push from the back brought me back to this world.

I moved and sat on a square few stairs below. I looked up again at the shivling, a sight unforgettable. It ever lives in my memory. Oft and on, in my vacant hours, it flashes before my mind and gives me immense joy. All shivlings that I was fortunate enough to visit faded before this majestic figure.

I sat there for some time, continually looking at the shivling. Thoughts ran within me, "continual and persistent efforts made in any direction are bound to succeed. Why then I should not try to move on a spiritual path that would take me out of all fears and help me to remove at least some human woes." Shivers ran through my body and I took a vow to act accordingly. I then saw two birds fluttering about the cave. I remembered the story mentioned in religious books about this place. Once Lord Shiv came with his wife Parvati to this place. She asked Shiv, "Lord there is so much of pain and misery in the world. Tell me how it can be eradicated." Lord finding the place lonely started narrating how men could get relief. Meanwhile Parvati went off to sleep and instead two men hiding there heard what the Lord said. When Shiv became aware of the situation, he cursed them and turned them into birds. The same can be seen fluttering about at this time. I was fortunate to see them at this time and they told me the secret that they had heard, the secret to bliss.

"Listen life is to give and not to take; Life is to live".

❑

Old Age

There is a growing feeling that happiness peaks at eighty. Are these the best days? I questioned few old ones whom I knew and the answer from them was yes, a big YES. It is often said that younger years are the best of one's life. But a new study reveals that people actually become happier when they grow older. Scholars doing research on this topic have come to the conclusion that happiness grows after middle age, when people start growing old, easily eclipsing the earlier years and peaking as late as eighties. An easing sense of responsibilities of middle age combined with maturity and ability to focus on things that one wishes to concentrate on and enjoy combine to make old age far more enjoyable than one might expect. This is immensely increased by having good health, a stable income, and good relationships all round. The researchers claim.

"From the mid-forties, people become more cheerful and optimistic reaching maximum in their late seventies or eighties." This is the observation made by Professor Lewis Wilbert, who led the study.

When I think of old age, I am reminded of an interesting story, which brings out my point very clearly. A handsome, healthy young elephant by the name of Heera was the king's pride. Whenever the king went out in public, his procession always had Heera, on whose back he sat. Heera was his favourite and for this very reason he was looked after with care and concern. In the procession, Heera carrying the king on his back, would walk proudly, with a charming gait, accompanied by a musical band that brought out a sweet melody which vibrated the atmosphere and announced loudly that the king was arriving. But then with the passing of time, Heera lost his looks and vigour. It was proclaimed that he was getting old and soon was moved to sulk in the corner of a compound. It so happened that one day, while moving slowly around, he fell into a ditch but instead of making an effort to get out Heerá just sat. A feeling had strongly overtaken him that he was not meant to make any effort. He had grown old and so pushed aside to sit. This very feeling is so frustrating. People noticed Heera and ran to save him. All efforts to pull him out failed, when finally the master who trained him was called for. He ordered the band to be played. On hearing the band, Heera opened his eyes started moving his head. The music grew louder, Heera stood up fast and bounced out of the ditch.

What is true of Heera is true of human beings. The very feeling that one has gone old, brings in frustration. The thought that he had grown old and that he had been pushed aside by the society as worthless is defeating. Psychologically he becomes sad and much disturbed. Feeling of desperation overtakes him and gradually with the type of treatment that he faces from the loving and all those around, he loses the courage to live. The new situations and disappointments that follow are hard to bear. All round he sees loneliness and gloom. Life changes drastically from excitement to boredom. You were too busy once and activities all round involved you. You got up in the morning saying to yourself "Oh, I have so many important things to do" and you busied yourself with vigour and enthusiasm. Now you get up and there is an utter blank before you. No enthusiasm, no hurry you can go off to sleep again. You moved on once with hope and courage but now you can sit with discouragement accompanied with only memories of the past.

You are told at your workplace, "Tomorrow is your farewell." A wave of shock runs within you. A sense of sheer desperation overtakes you "I am still so strong that I can conveniently go ahead, perhaps with better understanding and more experience. Why am I asked to step out." But soon comes the reply "You have to accept the rule that at sixty you are old and must quit and move out from the flow of the social activities." He does it and a psychological conflict goes on within him "What am I to do from the next day after I am garlanded and told by those who had assembled that they would miss me a lot. Who will miss whom is now the question." He goes out and sits idle at home trying hard to see his future. One day, with great enthusiasm he visits his workplace. He is hoping that he would get a warm welcome from his colleagues and subordinates. He is sad to hear the hissing sound of pity from all the sides "He has recently retired. All are busy with their work and no one really shows any interest in him. Even chawkidar shows little respect. This was the very place wherein his entrance created commotion. "Sir is coming" was the subdued noise all round. All is over. He must learn to accept all this. Old age has brought only insults and injuries. He must suffer with a smile. Old age enters with a bang too hard to bear. It is not only humiliating but almost killing a person. He must now choose a corner and sit like Heera. This is his fate now.

Old age is there even before one begins to feel the loss of physical strength. It pulls down a person heavily. Psychologically he is shattered and emotionally highly depressed. He runs hither and thither to find some other job that would engage him at least as long as he has the strength to do it. But no, from all sides comes the same echo, "Sorry, you are sixty, and we have nothing for you." This is the situation confronting all the old. Disappointed he sits with little hopes. It is a very sore point in old age. But the trouble does not end up here. More shocks are in waiting for him. Blows from his own son, his very loving son. It brings him to a dismal state.

It is only a very small section of the society that welcomes the old age. They are the ones who find in retirement, a time to rest from the hectic activities of life. They look forward to this time to pursue activities of their interest, for which they found little or no time during their tenure of service. They travel, go to visit shrines, go out for sight-seeing and are happy to be peacefully enjoying nature. They have earned enough to stand independently. The old age is then a comfortable time and looks bright. Watch the pair that now looks only to the company, to the togetherness and to the warmth of each other. Of course they have made sufficient provisions for themselves. Look at the old man who lovingly opens the umbrella for his old rugged wife to save her from the heat of the sun. The wife had never enjoyed such loving affection from her husband. He was ever in a hurry to leave for his office. Little acts of kindness and of love bring the joy of closeness and warmth that they had never experienced before. The wife now enjoys the attention because there is no hurry and worry of the office. They sit together for long hours to talk and agree with each other. Life blooms as never before. The empty path of the garden welcomes them, slowly as they stroll together carefully holding each other. They walk leisurely and peacefully, enjoying the cool breeze of the early morning, scented by the flowers growing around the path. They smile and look at each other. Their silent looks speak loudly, "How nice to be old and to be together. " Both are happy as one gives attendance to the other. Both are lucky thrilled in" the company of each other.

But this is not the story of the old in general. You may say these are only exceptions. Old are growing in numbers, perhaps because of better medical facilities available now. They form a good chunk of the population and need special care and attention. Let me put them under various groups:

1. The very rich, further pampered by rich sons staying abroad.
2. Old with sufficient money to support them but left alone with no one to share their woes.
3. Economically weak.
4. Economically bankrupt and physically weak.

In this first category come those who have earned enough and are rich. Their qualified sons have found good jobs abroad. They are also earning well. In their fondness for the parents they send all types of gadgets to see them comfortable and happy. They are living in huge bungalows. For security there are attendants and guards. I see them coming out for their morning walks well cared for, as servants walk behind them holding umbrellas to protect them from the changing weather. Though surrounded by all luxuries, they are still subject to human nature. Compelled by it they feel so lonely and unhappy. They run for company if they find one. After the stroll they sit down at a central place to hear what others have to say, and talk about their own experiences. He is so fond of others as others are fond of him. The old in their exchange of thoughts find this time as the best. The question arises why they are not happy with money in abundance to support them. Their loneliness defeats them and all the gadgets to amuse them lie in waste all round. Why money fails to make them happy? This is a big question that needs to be looked into.

In the second category come those old who preferred not to marry for this meant to them encroachment to their freedom. But as the old age appears and they have no sons and daughter to care for them they feel the pinch. They have no security and no one to share their thoughts, Also under this come those who are unlucky to lose their partner because destiny so decides for them. They now wade through without any one to share their joys and sorrows. The old age then becomes a curse as they look around and find no sympathizers. Young find them fussy and run away at their very sight. Life changes drastically. It is the presence of someone close to you that always gives great relief. Sharing gives strength. Your sorrows and pain diminish. You cheer up with encouragement that comes up from the other. With no such person you feel lost, unhappy, depressed and bewildered as the old age makes it appearance.

In the third category come those who are not so well off as the first two. Economically, they are weak and do not have enough to fall back upon. They cannot afford to live alone and need the strength and the security of the young. Life is a movement and they have moved a long distance giving all to the young in the hope that they would be looked after when their turn comes. The turn does come but are the young mindful of their duties? The modern society provides the answer. He had only one son, both too fond of each other. In this fondness the father who had constructed a house taking great pains, registers the house in the name of his son, for he is all in all for him, "You are my security and my happiness so all is yours" said the father.

"Yes dad" comes the sweet reply.

But soon he brings in a daughter-in-law, feeling highly elated that together they will be the happiest. But more you run after happiness, more happiness will run off from you. The father stands bewildered by the treatment of his son and in utter despondency he walks out of his own house that he made with dreams of hope and trust. Old age is itself a problem, why other problems are added to it, he wonders as he walks out to join an old home for peace for the tormented soul. The fact that the demand for the old homes is ever on increase speaks loudly of old men and of old age and the place they occupy in the modern society.

In the last group come those who are financially zero and do not know where to run away. All are miserable but the last is the worse amongst all. The old woman has not even the right to sit in the corner. Doubly bent she needs to run about doing errands that are ordered by the sweet daughter-in-law. All must work. That is the motto. Old pa is taking a bucket, walking slowly, scared that he might not hit against a vehicle, is seen moving carefully and cautiously towards the milk dairy. Such is the plight of the old, almost breaking the heart of an onlooker what to say of the one who undergoes all this and stands stunned. No one is there to take them out of their misfortunes. Only they have learnt to say "All is well, let it be."

A mother too proud of her two sons, whom she had to bring up alone, because of the early death of her husband, could find no home from either in her old age. One son got married into a rich family, so felt insulted in keeping an old, poor mother. The other married to a poor working girl and being himself a clerk found no means to keep her. But on the advice of his wife he took her to look after the children and attend to household jobs. She did all with great affection. But slowly as she was getting old, she got ill and was bed-ridden. For long she had served them but they could not tolerate her lying down sick and in a state where she was unable to serve them. So one day as she lay unconscious, the son picked her up and took her to the crossing near his elder brother's bungalow, laid her on the ground of the street and quietly ran off giving a call to his brother, " your mother is now at your doorstep lying unconscious." The brother as usual did not bother. She lay there at the mercy of the third party that might take pity on her.

This is no story but a real incident. I can add many such cases that are coming up every now and then. It shows the apathy of children towards the old. A gloomy old age stares and seems to lose all confidence in its own children. Old age is approaching fast and one seems to be getting suspicious of his own sons. In life you had walked a long distance, it is time to stop and think what can be the best for you. The alternatives are few. One can either revolt or accept or cry out aloud that all is not going the right way. Everything seems to be moving and changing fast. You are a witness watching the play but regretting your losing energies. Poor old exhausted you fail to think what is best for you. You are gripped with fears and stand paralyzed. You were after the quest of peace and a restful life in old age, instead there is only depression and desperation. Old men now know well that they have little or no assurances from their children, yet get trapped into odd situations as emotions bind them. But the intelligent ones move with understanding and proper planning. They save enough for a dignified old age. Their anticipative fears make them to keep a balance.

Money may be there for convenience but to be happy, the old have to look in some other direction. You get up in the morning and see an utter blank for the day. There is no enthusiasm. The lively past was so cheerful. It is a strong, though a silent link that further disturbs your mind. But still I feel all is not lost if you could only change your attitude towards life. You could not prevent a bolt from the blue that fell and paralyzed the life at Leh. In the same way, you cannot prevent the inevitable end in your life, the old age. But you can face this big challenge without being incapacitated by a sense of despair. You look to this time with fear and doubts. You need only to transform your mind. What counts is your attitude to old age. But this has to be done willingly, understanding well why it is necessary to do so.

You have so far been dominated by ego. With ego you lashed out when someone insulted or even disagreed with you. It was your ego that made you to judge others and control others. You approved all your actions right or wrong. But now with old age you begin to curtail your ego and accept the situations, however bitter they may be. This comes because of your mature understanding. With ego subdued you learn to accept your flaws and your position and so move accordingly. The change in attitude comes willingly.

Your ego had kept you aloof and away from all. An old man went to a sadhu and asked him, “Is there any way to get out of the miseries of old age?” The sadhu replied and went away, “Turn to your master, the God.” The old thought seriously and felt that he has got the right answer. So far he had served a number of masters at variance with him but now he has to serve only one master kind and close to him. Motivated he went ahead and found real happiness in his life.

Now with one master, you move with a strong feeling that He attends to your grievances and gives you courage to move in the right direction and with the right attitude. You then start taking interest in spiritual practices and move to identify yourself with soul than with ego. Old age does all this and much more for you. The chain of desires kept you shackled to the world and you found it very difficult to break it. But once you break it, if you turn to

God, you are free. The longings disappear and there is no more grief and no more disappointments that come from longings.

The stream in which you were flowing so far is diverted in another direction of peace and elation. The life of spiritual existence is essentially different from the life of a conditioned mind of egoistic desires. You cease to be motivated by personal interest. By your own efforts you set your matters right. You need a strong and good loving hand to hold you. God provides one. It is God that has made you to run and now it is your turn to run for Him. And once you are motivated with the Divine, the Spirit functions through you. You no longer face the difficulties that you were facing so far. You do not get up frustrated in the morning. You greet the morning with a cheer and a warm welcome. There is excitement and no more boredom. All that you needed you find in His company and in His consolation. There is happiness as you evolve spiritually.

Old age is the time to understand that enough days have been spent thinking of the body only. The other part namely the soul has been completely neglected. You are being called at this stage to turn to the soul and be one with God. To my mind old age spiritualizes naturally: This is the time when finding no consolation around and being in a state of sheer helplessness one looks to God as his last resort. In Him he finds a close companion and help.

"My soul was dark with a stormy riot" said the old man, "but now with my old age I have resolved to stop complaining. I move with things as they are". Old age learns to be content. It is this attitude that makes the difference. It is the right attitude, derived only through spiritual experiences. Old age then looks up with a confidence and with a smile. There is no need to look with scare at the old age. When the brain burns, it takes a turn, and every moment a new song rises out of the fire, the mists are cleared, and a new vitality makes you spring up the new steps before you, as you now walk enriched in the service of God and mankind.

❑

Are You Depressed?

Words that have gained prevalence in the modern society are depression, stress and tension. You will hear your friend or your neighbour say, "Depression had overtaken me. I was under great stress out of which I could not come out for long." An acquaintance whom you happen to meet and ask him why he was looking so unwell would reply, "I am undergoing depression."

Saurabh had become the victim of depression. He worked hard to please his master. Instead he gets rebukes. Now his thoughts circle only round him and he is much worried about himself. He conjectures odd results for himself and goes into depression. Instead of taking a positive attitude that he should work harder, he becomes an easy prey to futile thoughts and goes into depression. He wanted events to go in his own way. If he had worked hard, the master should praise him. Instead he got annoyed, why? He feels that he is a helpless victim and pities himself and goes into depression.

Shanti was very much oppressed by her husband. She had to live in a way that her husband wanted. Things went against her ethics but acceptance was her only lot. She was not allowed to go to her parents with whom she was much attached. Instead of creating in herself courage to fight against the injustice, she accepted it, suffered and went into depression. She, out of fear, got ugly thoughts about her future and succumbed to the deadly disease of depression.

A lady went into depression because her husband started neglecting her. He pampered her before but now he is interested in other things. Unnecessary fears are cooked up resulting in depression.

The bad behaviour of a dutiful son ever since he got married sends the mother into depression. She does not look around and see that all mothers are facing the same situation, only the degrees differ. Why is it that she feels that things have gone wrong only in her case. Her fears of future send her into depression.

A businessman lost his money when his business failed. He went into depression. A student failed and was under depression. On the appointment of a new secretary, the husband was no longer giving attention to his wife that she was getting before and she falls an easy prey to heavy depression. A daughter-in-law goes into depression because of the ill treatment meted out to her by the mother-in-law.

The whole problem with the depressive persons is that they seek to count that which they do not have. The gains that they are enjoying do not count for them at all. Men with plenty have no joy over things they possess. They suffer from fears of what they might lose. He is like a person who is sitting in a hall where lovely music is going on, but instead of finding peace and joy in the symphony, his mind is busy thinking how the world had hurt him. The depressed person usually goes back to the past and finds the present not the way he had looked forward to.

Another reason why we are overpowered by depression is the lack of courage. Fortitude is needed to overcome adversity. No one has time for others, A depressive mind needs that others should bleed with him. Why should they? If you laugh, the world will join you, but if you weep, you weep alone. Depression is self-defeating. You have to develop courage and stand for yourself in times of adversity and in this you are alone. Do not justify yourself.

I had a close relation of mine, a rich lady who lost her husband in a road accident. The thought that she would now be without any financial aid and so had to put a poor face to show to the world went into a fit of depression. She had two small children. The husband had hardly made any provision. She lost her courage to live and in a fit of depression went to the market to get poison. In the market an old acquaintance told her of many ways she could earn, even though she was uneducated. She did not pay any heed because her depression had already chalked a way out for her. When she returned, the little ones came running and lovingly embraced her. She looked at them and thought of the future. She felt pity for the little ones, She threw to the winds her thoughts of what the neighbours would say, she started cooking and packing tiffin boxes for the office goers of an office near her house. She earned enough and soon started making huge profits as her subscribers increased in large numbers. She was in a position to give good education to her two sons. They grew up to occupy high posts. She threw her depression to the winds, and was determined to succeed and not to succumb to her misfortune. See what havoc depression could have done? Ended three lives? It is your courage with which you can fight depression. It is determination on your part to succeed that can take you out of this terrible disease.

You need to be self-critical. To develop this disposition you have to change your attitude. A changed attitude can bring a transformation in the very course of your life. We cannot change our nature, but definitely we can change our attitude towards happenings. It is the attitude that greatly matters. A guru had two disciples. Guru asked them to observe the world and give him their report. The one who saw only the day and its brightness, considered the world wonderful and bright. The darkness of night did come, so what? It was soon overcome by hopes and light of the coming morning. The other disciple who saw only night and its darkness reported that the world is a hopeless place.

The brightness of the day lost its value when he saw that it was darkness that always preceded and followed it. The darkness was disgusting. One saw only the nights and darkness, the other saw only light and brightness. It is the change of the attitude that can make an immense difference. Milton has rightly said, "It is the mind of the man, that can make heaven of hell and hell of heaven." With the right attitude towards men and events, the whole world will change for you and there will be no more depression.

Positive thinking is the need of the hour. What if I have failed? It does not lead to the conclusion that I will always fail. Instances are numerous where positive thinking has been found to be of great help. "Let me try again and this time I am bound to succeed." Instill this feeling within you and you are sure to succeed. If you give up after distress you are heading for depression. Learn the lesson from an ant which tries to go up, falls down, and yet begins to climb again. It falls many times, but that does not deter it to try again and again until at last it does succeed. Depression is nothing but giving up. Let not your failure make you an easy prey to depression.

What is depression? Why do we fall an easy prey to it? These are some of questions that confront us. To my mind it comes to mean only one thing, the fear that the things are not going to happen in the way I like, the fear of what I cannot see. It is 'I' that becomes the centre around which everything rotates. Ego becomes the root cause. Motivated by fear, we are tempted to create situations in which we put ourselves and then suffer. These people are living in a self-created world where they are the poor sufferers. The rest of the world outside their own does not exist. They are unaware of their surroundings and what is happening to others. Their only concern is what they should have got and what they have lost. They seem to project in their minds ugly situations for which they are not responsible and not finding any proper solutions they hurt their ego.

So what is required of us in all cases of depression is a quiet surrender to the Lord. A spiritual power can be of great help to eradicate this disease. Doctors and their pills can be of little help. The root cause has to be treated. In the battle of Kurukshetra, Arjun was under heavy depression and he had refused to fight. The only cure for Arjun was when he surrendered himself to the Lord. He then, not only got strength to fight against injustice but also got rid of the feeling of 'I, "me', and 'mine'. Listen to the Lord, follow Him and the whole world will change for you. Accept Him with a readiness and a smile for He alone can put His hand forward and hold you and bring you out of the mire in which you have got yourself stuck.

❑

Courage in Adversity

Adversities are the challenges, the difficult times that you face in your life. They may broadly be taken under the following heads:

1. Those caused by natural calamities, like famines, earthquakes, floods, tidal waves, hurricanes and volcanoes etc.
2. Those caused by diseases and infections. Those caused by war at home or abroad.
3. Those that occur due to the mental attitude like anger, jealousy, and anxieties.

These are mainly the type of challenges that you face in your life. Some may face only few while many adversities may be in the lot of others. But life as it stands means challenges. A storm is an essential part of the sailors who are out sailing in the waters. Overtaken by a storm sailors may behave in either of the three ways:

1. He may give himself up to the flow of the storm and sail downstream and become miserable.
2. He may at least try to sail his boat upstream though he may have to face problems that might upset him.
3. He may with his sharp intelligence use the harsh blowing winds for his benefit. He would adjust all negative situations for his good. He would harness the wind power to overcome

the power of the water. He would then be successful in moving upstream.

Life is a stream that flows and storms are an essential part of it. To what category of the sailors you belong to, needs to be seen. Men compared to sailors as above can be put as:

1. Those who make hell of their sufferings.
2. Those who accept their sufferings and try hard to minimize its effect. As they cannot change, they accept it as God's will.
3. Those who rise above, determined to overcome their adversities and make them opportunities.

Life means challenges. There may be some fortunate ones while others may not be so. But life as it stands means challenges. You need to go through them in some form or the other. It is not necessary that you become an angel going through adversities. You can also become a devil. It is how you react to these adversities that you become what you are. But usually I see that the best in you comes out in going through adversities. In that way the challenges that you face brings out the best in you. So they ought to be considered as blessings. In your prayers you need to say "thank you adversity."

Why fear challenges. Just think, are you in a position to take off these challenges from your life? You have no control over them. Can you ward off the natural calamities that might take place? No, you have no control over natural calamities like earthquakes, floods, heavy rains, hurricanes, tidal waves, volcanoes and the like. You cannot say with certainty that no disease will overtake you that might not take a serious turn. With certainty you cannot say that you will not lose your job. You can lose your home, your wealth, or someone on whom your entire dependence rests. You cannot even be sure that one who goes out in the morning will safely be back at night. You cannot prevent death from coming to you or to your loved ones. So challenges are there for you at every step.

Uncertainties are all around you and you have to move on with them. What is important is your own attitude towards them. How you react to what happens to you is what will give shape to your life and character. Happiness or unhappiness does not depend on what happens to you but how you react to what happens to you in your life. If you can only change your thoughts you can change your world. You need to welcome anything whatsoever that comes in your life prepared to overcome any adversity that comes your way.

"My life is very hard" someone told me.

"Compared to what" I asked him.

"As compared to yours" was his quick rejoinder.

"For me, my life has been very hard, only you do not realize it" I retorted "Has it been a bed of roses for any one?" I asked.

You have to accept the truth that life is not an iPod where you can hear the music of your choice. It is a radio wherein you have to adjust yourself to be happy with anything that comes your way.

Try to welcome every morning with a smile. Look on the new day as a special gift from the creator. Believe me, here is another opportunity to start with something you missed yesterday. Let your thoughts be of success and positive thinking. Do not waste time. Today will never happen again. Do not waste it with false start or no start at all. Since you alone are responsible for your thoughts, it is you alone who can change what and how you think. You will change them when you want to change them. Therefore think only those thoughts that bring you health and happiness.

It is you who is creating problems and suffering under its pressure. It is not the problem that is giving you pain as what you are making out of it by your thoughts. If you are suffering, the only way to come out of the trouble would be by your own positive thoughts. It reminds me of the story of the monk who carried a mirror with himself wherever he went. A priest noticed it and thought to himself, "This monk must be vain that he has to carry the mirror around all the time. He should not worry about the looks on the outside, it is what is inside that counts." So the priest went up to the monk to shame him and asked "Why do you always carry the mirror?" The monk pulled the mirror out of his bag and pointed to the priest. Then he said "I use it in the times of troubles. I look at it and it shows me the source of my trouble as well its solution."

Challenges are very much a part of life. But you look at them with fear. Many of you are unprepared for life's challenges and you tend to crack down under its pressure. But just think are you in a position to end these challenges? You can cry and wail over the events that happen to you. You may tend to accept them as you feel you cannot change them. But you can also face them with a determination not only to overcome but to rise above them to make them opportunities. It is you who has to make the choice. A fear always lurks in your mind as to what the future holds for you. It is up to you to face adversities either with courage or with despair.

I have put three categories of men and women and you belong to one of them. In the first category come those who by their own thoughts make their way of life miserable. Your bondage is your own making. And you are yourself forging the chains around yourself and living unhappily. You make adversities tenfold and suffer or bend under its pressure. You suffer from depression, anger and jealousy. Your problems are self-created and solutions based on hasty decisions.

I know of a friend of mine who was always full of smiles, very social and friendly, very cheerful, laughing, talking, moving around making friends She gave birth to a mentally challenged child. She changed drastically. It was really so sad to see her. No smiles, no jokes, and no moving about. As if this was not enough she lost her husband in an accident. Her thoughts, the way she talked was so depressive. One who was willing to take part in each and every activity refused to think about them anymore. She became an absolute recluse. She happened to sit with me once and I asked her "What has gone wrong with you, Sheila? You are killing yourself by your own thoughts and behaviour."

She replied sadly "Now no one talks to me and no one wants to come to my place."

"So what you have so many interests otherwise which you can pursue." I replied.

"As people hate my company, I hate them."

"These are entirely your thoughts as you conjure them." I said.

As I tried to bring her out of her damaging thoughts, she argued, "Are all the pains in life meant for me alone?"

"But you are not counting the immense blessings that you have, my dear". I said, as I tried to argue out. "You have money power. You have other two sons and a daughter so well placed and all doing so well in life. Why adversities should hit you to change your way of thinking about your life." I pleaded with her.

She then replied in a very sad tone "I look around and see no one has problems like me. I am being singled out by God for all these. I have broken down completely. Others instead of having any sympathy for me hate me. So I hate them all."

I tried to help her out, but anger, jealousy and despair coloured her thoughts and doomed her. She had chained herself so badly with her negative thoughts that she suffered from despair and became a recluse. Life became burdensome to her by her way of thinking. She forgot to smile and often I saw her with tears only, sitting alone with her child.

William Cowper, a great poet of the eighteenth century is an example from English literature of how a poet with great potentialities could not achieve much because of the malady he suffered from time to time. He desired something on which he could not insist upon. He became weak and helpless and became a prey to his own thinking and suffered from bouts of depression. In his own thoughts he became weak and helpless. What he desired he suppressed giving way to what he should not have been. This conflict was the cause of his depression. Because of this, a poet who could have risen high, was just an obsolete figure in literature. He could not realize his own potential as he lost his self confidence in his own ability and failed to become a great poet.

My neighbour, a young man by the name of Kailash, was a successful businessman who had met with great success in his work. All of a sudden he had bad luck and a severe setback in his business. As usual his creditors started worrying him. A very optimistic fellow with suddenness changed completely. I happened to meet him and was quite surprised to see a complete change in his thought process.

"I am much worried about my future." he said

"Why worry, work hard, think in a positive way and this failure itself be a stepping stone for success in the times to come. We learn only by our mistakes" I said.

"Oh no! a business man is a realistic man and always calculates his future and my future worries me as I look at it."

"Change your thought process then. You are unnecessarily magnifying your troubles as you are confused. You are loading your future with your negative thoughts. It is obvious that you are scared of your future. Why you do not try to understand that these thoughts are there because of your recent setback. Overrule them and walk ahead with a firm belief that you will be careful next time and you are sure to succeed." I argued.

He listened quietly but with little change in his expression. He had chained himself so badly with his thoughts that next morning I got the news that he was found hanging by the ceiling fan. His suffering was his own activity, his complete voluntary activity, for in business ups and downs are always there well known to anyone who enters it.

It so happened that I bought a house for myself from a gentleman who had planned to live in this house with his wife after retirement. In life he was very happy living with his wife and two sons. The wife was very much devoted to her husband and he in turn loved her and was very fond of her. He got a promotion in his job and became the director of a creative agency. As a part of his job he had to go around with young and pretty girls. He had no fancy for them and if he had to spend time with them it was essential as a part of his work in the office. But the wife read it in her own way. Everything looks yellow to a jaundiced eye. So did every action of her husband looked to her as one deceiving her. At every turn she felt that the husband did not care for her. No longer did he love her. She was not getting the same attention from him as he gave to her before his promotion. She argued within with her thoughts that he had gone fed up of her as there were smarter and younger girls giving him company. If he hurried up because of some appointment she felt that no longer he relished her company. She became a case of severe depression and untimely took to bed. Chained by her thoughts she died an early death making the entire family miserable.

A bright student of mine was quite taken aback when she got poor marks in the examination. Her world became gloomy with her disappointing thoughts. "All had high expectation from me, they would be shocked to see my result. I will have to hang my head down with shame

How can I face them?" This is what she told me when she came to me as she was intimate with me and would often come to me for advice and help. I argued with her, "So what if by chance you have stumbled once, on other occasions you have already shown your caliber. Your failure will make you extra careful and I can assure you that next time you will come out with flying colours. Leave your negative thoughts and move ahead with confidence that you will be the winner." But she continued to harp on her thoughts that had chained her mind and her heart. Her own thinking had made her to feel that she had disappointed others and so she had no right to live. In her confused way of thinking she took a hasty decision, took poison at night and died.

These few examples above are of those sailors whose boats went downstream with the strength of the storm taking them with its flow and finally creating great havoc and destruction for the sailor and their boats.

In the second category are those sailors who at least make some effort and try to sail their boats upstream. They may live quite frustrated in life, but they show a brave face to the world. They make a compromise with the situations as they appear in life. They accept things that are much to their dislike. They smile though their hearts bleed.

Lovers discover that their union is impossible. They react in different ways.

Some drown themselves, some run away but few accept the harsh verdict of others. Those who drown themselves or those who run away may be put in the first category but those who sacrifice their own happiness and have to bow down to the wishes of others may be put in the second category. They live with disgust but put a smile on their faces. Their thoughts give them courage and their way of thinking make it possible to accept things which they feel they cannot change. So acceptance is the only answer. They accept the situation as God's will. Happiness is not in their lot but their thoughts tell them that if others are happy he need not think about his own happiness alone. They argue, life has to go on and the best is to live for others.

I know of a poor boy, by the name of Ramesh, who was very bright in his studies and would come out in every class with bright colours. He was very poor and circumstances did not allow him to carry on with his studies. Had he been allowed to complete his studies he would have competed for a high post and would have surely got into it. But parents were struggling in poverty for a good long time and had great hopes from this son. So with minimum qualification that he had, he appeared in the competition held for the post of a head clerk and was selected. He accepted the job and brought in money for the family. It meant a loss to them, for those who got respite from hunger and pain. But with Ramesh a feeling of disgust and frustration always remained. He accepted the situation as his destiny.

Natural calamities take place. All round there is nothing but destruction. But out of the ruins they pick up the threads and start building their new homes. All is swept away but combined with pain and frustration is the strong feeling that this has to go on and they must accept it as it has to go with the place. They accept it as God's will and as a part of their destiny. Natural calamity is the adversity which is accepted as an essential part of life in that region. Something that you cannot change you have no other way but to accept it as bad luck.

In the third category are those who face the adversities with a determination not only to overcome them but treat them as opportunities to rise high. They are the sailors who with their intelligence harness the wind power to overcome the power of water successfully and take the ship upstream. You ought to live to the belief that you can turn the world around. You need to be confident that you can make a better tomorrow. I would ask you that if you are not going to be better tomorrow than today then for what do you need tomorrow for? Tomorrow ought to be looked forward to with thoughts of hope and encouragement. You need to give a fitting challenge to your adversities only then your life can bloom. Your thoughts are your guide. Your worst enemies cannot harm you as much as your thoughts. Develop your mind to keep your unguarded thoughts off. Create a confidence in yourself that the worst cannot defeat you. You are, where thoughts will bring you and you will be where your thoughts take you. Start now, for it is never too late, to think of only those thoughts that bring you happiness. I have learned with my own experience that if you advance confidently in the direction of your own belief and endeavour to live a life which you have imagined, you are sure to meet with unexpected success. Such thoughts are the touchstone of your character. It is your choice and not chance that determines your destiny. Face bravely and not fear your challenges. Determined ones are the successful ones.

In a remote town of Africa, two businessmen went to find out if they could get some business there. Both were shoemakers. The ground of this place was quite tough yet no one wore any type of shoes. They were quite comfortable moving about bare-footed. One came back thinking as no one was putting on shoes there was no opportunity for him over there. He came back disappointed. The other one thought that he would go about and show men there the advantages of putting on shoes. His ideas clicked well on the inhabitants of that place and he made very good business there. He made heavy profits. While one saw adversity as adversity the other opportunity through adversity. All depends on your thought process. One thought negatively, while the other thought and reacted positively and won.

Braille was a boy, who while playing with his hammer hit himself badly. The hammer went off from his hand and directly hit him on his face. He instantly became blind as the hammer hit him on his eyes. Though he became blind it did not deter him from pursuing his education. Eventually, he developed a system that is even now used by blind to read. His disaster did not defeat him. Instead he, with determination fought it out to create something new and useful. His adversity did not discourage him, it only became an opportunity for him. I would say that it is very important for you to have thoughts that would make you to endeavour.

It is best for you to be situated in this third category. Ganga Ram was a poor boy of a village. He had dreams for himself to become an engineer and do something useful for the village that was hard hit by diseases. He worked hard and appeared for the post of a junior engineer. He cleared the written test and was called for an interview. He walked a long distance as he could not afford any conveyance. The place had only one seat and that was for the examiner. The examiner got late and he had to stand for a good long time. He thought of sitting for a while. He sat on the examiner's seat and went off to sleep as he was very tired walking a long distance. The examiner entered and was furious seeing him on his chair. He shouted for the attendant and told him to throw out Ganga Ram from his room and then called the clerk and told him that he should never be given any opportunity to sit for this post. Poor Ganga Ram bearing all these insults, with tears in his eyes came back home. But he was unwilling to give up. Resolved not to accept defeat he applied for a higher post in the same office. He worked hard, harder than he could imagine. He sat by the roadside under the pale lamplight for the whole night to finish reading parts of the book that he borrowed and was given for the night only. He was selected. He worked harder in the office and got quick promotions for his excellent hard work. Later on his works were recognized by higher British authorities and he was awarded the title of "Sir". He had not forgotten his own village. He made a hospital for them as so many go unattended and die. It goes by his own name. One of the famous hospital of Delhi that goes as "Sir Ganga Ram Hospital". It is a hospital for those who are suffering from illness and diseases but more than that it is a hospital for all who are suffering from adversities and fear of adversities. Here is a pointer to all those who are scared of adversities and lack determination to confront bravely all misfortunes that come on their way. Keep a sure guard on your thought process. You are never so weak as to be defeated by adversities. Enemies cannot harm you as much as your thoughts. Develop your mind, keep your unguarded thoughts off. You can then only come to a point where there is happiness for you. Just relax and walk in life with thoughts that cheer you up and encourage you to take steps towards a destination that you have always longed for.

An emperor, who had dreams of becoming a great king, once suffered a severe defeat. In thoughts of depression, he felt like giving up and killing himself. His negative thoughts were overpowering him. But once as he lay on his bed vacantly looking at the wall, he saw an ant trying to climb up the small wall to enjoy sugar that was spread on the top of it. It climbed but after some distance it fell down. The efforts were made repeatedly but it could make little progress when it fell down at every turn, only making a little progress than before. The little thing did not lose hopes and tried a number of times till it reached to the top to enjoy the sugar. The emperor watching this sight thought that if this small ant is not discouraged by its failures why should a great conqueror, like him lose hopes. He got up and fought again and won. His thoughts led him to victory. Actually, it is your thought process that leads you towards the onward march to overcome adversity and make you a successful man.

Many such examples can be cited from life where determination to realize the mission has been responsible for the success of the person. Enormous adversities confront them but by their thoughts they have overcome them all. Mahatma Gandhi was a frail ordinary person, who confronting all types of adversities, could rise up to provide a strong leadership to a large nation. He could bring together all men and women under one banner. A strong force he created to drive the Britishers out. His thoughts, his vision, his determination and his endeavors made him what he is, the Father of the Nation. His positive thoughts led him to free a nation from a foreign rule under which the country reeled for centuries. He fought with confidence and challenged every adversity that came his way.

It is best to belong to the third category. Your thoughts ought to be such that carry you successfully towards a happy goal. I would like to emphasize that you begin to die if negative thoughts accompany you. You need a conscious effort, with positive thoughts, to move on in the right direction, facing adversities with courage and confidence. Keep your unguarded thoughts off. These can harm you more than your bitter enemies. Let not the doubts and fears ever accompany you. Remember you were born to live and win. So let not the negative thoughts be your companion. Throw them far off and with confidence learn to face adversities giving them a brave challenge. Wish for the best. God has given you his own divine attributes. Remember Him and rise upto it.

Once Kunti, the mother of Pandavas told Lord Krishna, "I love my troubles and adversities more than my good times.'

Lord Krishna asked, "But why?"

Kunti replied, "I love your company, but you are by my side only when I am in trouble."

Lord Krishna smiled as he said, "I am always with you, but you remember to call me only when you are in problems."

So always keeping Him in mind and always remembering Him, we have to move ahead, smiling with confidence and repeating within ourselves that "I can defeat the worst."

I repeat, it is you who is your enemy. It is you who is going to beat yourself. It is you who conjures up monsters and shiver. It is you alone that is responsible for losing your self-confidence. It is your negative thinking that pulls you down. I may remind you that strength is never the result of winning. It is your struggles that develop your strength. It is only when you go through hardships and take a firm decision that at no point you are going to surrender, that is your real strength.

❑

Navaratri

Navaratri brings about a natural upsurge of energies in the human system. It is a time of rejoicing and celebrating. The very wind that blows gives out the message that there is peace. The message of Bhagwat Gita is that peace is required in this world torn with pain and confusion (2.70). Truly peace is needed, peace where only tensions prevail, peace in the mind of disturbed thoughts, peace in the heart torn with jealousy and greed and peace all around. Navaratri is the time when the vibrations in atmosphere give out a sweet memory of peace, rejoicing and happiness.

Traditionally this week that is celebrated all round, speaks of the good conquering the evil. This week is very special and looked forward with eagerness. Modern science has tried hard to give us ways and methods of how we can achieve peace. This is the goal they worked for. But the more it has tried, the more it has brought the world towards destruction, hatred and war. The need of the hour is the spiritual turn.

It is a week of longing, longing to know, longing to go deep into the spiritual process. We need to be aware and awake. So various situations are created to combine powerful meditation with celebration. It is a time that must keep us awake and alert. Alert for the values that it has awaken that behind the rejoicing there is something deep to understand and imbibe.

The One that is worshipped during this week is Durga Ma. She is the centre of attraction. There are so many ways of addressing

Her. Ambe, Kalyani, Rudrani, Maharani and Kali. All these are put with the word "Maya". It is only to bring out the Mother in the Divine. Our thoughts about Her take us out of all doubts as to what She stands for. She is the highest form of Power, yet She is the highest form of Love. She is very cruel to the evil, yet most loving to the good.

She is "Shakti", the great power that had finished the most dangerous demons Mahishasur, Shumbh-Nishumbh, Madhukaitabh and many others equally powerful. But we need to understand the relevance they have for us. We are confronted every day with more powerful demons than these, the demons of hatred, jealously, dishonesty, selfishness and apathy. These She stands to destroy, for we are Her children whom she loves and cares for. "Ratri" in Sanskrit stands for three types of pain, ethereal, mental and material. Navaratri brings peace to the three instruments namely body, mind and speech. All round we are engulfed in darkness, darkness created by our ego. She is light that diffuses all such darkness. There is everywhere celebrations and rejoicing in this week. But She needs to be understood in Her real self and Her real spirit. Let us not overlook this very important aspect.

Her power is recognized even by the Gods. In "Devi Bhaguatam" we are told how once sat in Samadhi, the great Lord Vishnu, Lord Brahma and Shankar who happened to see Him in this pose, questioned, "Lord of the universe what Samadhi are You sitting in? Whom do You worship? At your word, all function. You are the greatest of the great, yet here I find You at worship. Who is worthy of Your devotion, Narayana?" Vishnu answered with seriousness, "Brahma, indeed You create, I preserve and Rudra destroys the universe. Yet without Shakti, the three of us would be lost, and powerless. Maha Shakti, the Goddess, is the highest power of all and She animates the rest of us. There is none I know of who is higher than Parashakti and it is upon Her that

I meditate", replied Vishnu. Her greatness, Her power, Her ways cannot be compared to any.

At every turn, we hear Brahma saying, "only Mahamaya, the Devi can help us now. Let us pray to Her." Madhu Kaitabh attacked Brahma and the one who could come to His rescue was divine Ambe Ma to whom He prayed with intensity and reverence. Ma Durga, Mahamaya and Bhagwati stand very high in the estimation of all the Devas. They worship Her and at all times of trials and dangers, it is She who comes to their rescue. She is the creator, preserver and destroyer of this universe. She stands supreme.

For us, the worldly men, She is the one who can take us out of ignorance. She is the light which we are engulfed. "Devi is Kali and Durga. She is Saraswati that will dispel all darkness in which we are engulfed. "Devi is Kali and Durga and Mahalakshmi. She is Sati, Sita and Radha. She is mother of the universe, without Her animating power, Shiv becomes Shav (corpse)". All need Her and She is the great power behind all.

She is Divine who has also the divinity of Brahma, Vishnu and Mahesh. Once Indra was in great trouble as he with all other devas was vanquished by the great demon Mahishasur. He was one who could change himself in any form that he liked. He drove Indra and all devas out of heaven and sat on the seat of Indra. Thus driven out, Indra with all his companions, roamed on earth like common men. They were in a pitiable state. Not finding any other solution they came to a place where sat Brahma, Vishnu and Mahesh and narrated their plight. They heard their sorrow and were greatly annoyed by Mahishasur who had crossed all his limits. Their intense anger sparked out their tremendous energies. These mingled to form a strong, powerful light that shone so brightly in its brilliance that no light could withstand. It lighted up the entire atmosphere and challenged all around. Its brilliance had no parallel. This was none but Durga Ma, the destroyer of Mahishasur.

It is at this time of Navaratri, that we get into a feeling that She is very close to us. This is the time when we can set our goal, the goal to reach Her. If we can do that, and we walk steadily towards our aim, always keeping it as a top priority, we are sure to find shelter under Her loving care. Any step that keeps us away from our aim, should be treated as meaningless. If you are climbing a mountain, to reach the top, every step and all your energies are needed to reach the goal. Now if our aim is to reach Her, all our concentration and efforts are to be in that direction only. If our efforts are sincere and feelings intense we will definitely succeed. This is what I have realized in my own life.

I was disappointed many times, but I never lost heart. My thought often disturbed me and shook me from my path. But with all these I kept on walking ahead assured that someday She will accept me and She did. How else challenged from all sides by troubles and bouts of severe pain, I could continue to give a smile to the world and walk on as if nothing had happened to me and nothing had broken me. Often disturbed I got the courage to keep myself steady. My life has been a saga of pain, yet She has inspired me to take the worst with ease.

My immense faith in Ma Durga has given me lot of confidence, but I always pray that she could draw me still closer to Her:

Faith is essential in our lives. Let us put faith in someone, someone who is much higher than ourselves. Mata Durga has these attributes. We need to realize this and put our faith in Her. Her blessings are enormous and we are sure to get immense strength from Her. It will bring within us enormous change, both physical and spiritual. It is we who have put our hands on our eyes and cry that it is all dark. We have just to take that hand away to see the light.

Have you ever been just sitting somewhere and all of a sudden you feel like doing something nice for someone? That is Mata Ambe talking to you through the spirit. Have you ever been broken down and nobody seems to be around for you to talk to? That is where Mata wants you to talk to Her. There it is no chance in coincidence when you feel someone's hand round you to make you walk when you are faltering at every step. Have you received something which you desired from your heart? Have you been in pain physical or mental, out of which you see no way out? That is She passing you through tribulation to see a bright day. Her hand is everywhere and nothing is too little to let you know the truth that She is with you in many ways. Feel Her presence and feel it strongly during jubilations and celebrations of Navaratri, She is looking at you with smiling eyes so that you may not go away without making up your mind to come to Her finally.

Whether one is a monk or a householder, divine grace alone can save us from being deluded. We must take refuge in Mata for removing doubts, obstacles and surrender our ego with complete faith just as a child has in his mother. What destroys us is our ego. The minute we begin to feel that we have become great and important our fall begins. Madhu and Kaitabh, the demons, could not be defeated when they fought with Lord Vishnu. The war lasted for five thousand years. It could not be concluded as both parties were equally powerful. Lord Brahma observing this got much scared and prayed to Ma Durga to come to His rescue and make it possible that the demons could be defeated. Do you know what weapon She used to defeat them? It was the weapon of Ego. She made them to feel that they were really great, as Lord Vishnu, the great God, could not defeat them. The minute this sense of ego, their feeling of vanity overtook them, they were gone. In their pride, they told Lord Vishnu, "Come on, we are pleased by your strength to fight with us, so you can ask for a boon from us." Lord Vishnu replied, "I only wish that you may die at my hands." What strength and skill could not achieve was achieved by the ego, their sense of pride and they both died at Lord Vishnu's hand. So this ego is our arch-enemy and we need to be very careful. Tribulations and defeats will not destroy us but our fall is sure the minute we are overpowered by our ego. You may rise high by your efforts and determination but the minute you are overtaken by the feeling that you are great which makes you to look down upon others, be sure your bad time has begun. The only way to get rid of this feeling is a complete surrender to Ma Durga.

We must learn to experience the joy of becoming one with the infinite. Ramkrishna was one who neither possessed any bookish knowledge nor did he know any of the philosophies of religion. He knew only one language, the language of love. This is what he preached and practiced, the language of unconditional love for the Divine Mother which bridge the gulf between the mortals and immorality. The keynote of Ramkrishna's teachings begins, spreads and ends with the love for the Divine Ma. As ego is difficult to separate from a human body, the best course then would be to surrender it to the Divine. Let us look forward to the joy of becoming one with the Divine. But for us absolute surrender is difficult as we are enslaved by five senses. So the most effective spiritual method to be used is prayer. The Divine Mother is bound to respond to the call of Her children.

Call Her then, Navaratri is the time.

❑